Thank You, Everyone

Thank You, Everyone

A Lifetime of Gratitude in Letters

PAM JANIS

AVON BOOKS NEW YORK

AVON BOOKS, INC.
1350 Avenue of the Americas
New York, New York 10019

First Avon Books Trade Paperback Printing: April 1999

AVON TRADEMARK REG. U.S. PAT. OFF. AND IN OTHER COUNTRIES, MARCA REGISTRADA, HECHO
EN U.S.A.

Printed in the U.S.A.

OPM 10 9 8 7 6 5 4 3 2 1

In memory of, with gratitude to and for,
Howard K. Janis, Franny Borderud and George B. Rumsey

Thank
You,
Everyone

*"She is scared . . .
Scared to run out of time."*
—BONNIE RAITT

*P*reface

Most books begin with the author's thank-yous, then get to the story. This one begins with a story, then gets to the thank-yous.

Less than a month after my fortieth birthday, a day after what I thought of as my "Happy fortieth birthday" mammogram, my doctor called to tell me I had to come back for another one, "a closer look," he said.

The radiologist had found "a shadow" on one of my left films, and they needed to investigate.

This was a Friday, and the earliest possible day I could have my redo mammogram was Monday.

That gave me three days—and nights—to think about the possibilities. An alarmist by nature and heritage, I was sure this could only be bad news. That weekend was the start of the Jewish High Holidays; I'm sure my mother was flabbergasted to see me at *every* service.

I didn't tell her—alarmists never want to alarm anyone else—but I spent that weekend thinking about what I'd do if the news was bad.

I decided that I would write thank-you notes to all the people in my truly wonderful life, living or dead, who had helped shape it. When I thought about it, I realized that everything I'd ever done or loved had a special person attached to it, sometimes far back along a long and winding road of years and events, but there nonetheless. Whether sublime (learning to read), or ridiculous (eating grapefruit in sections, like an orange), every act or love in our lives was first taught, inspired, or encouraged by one person. How many of them have we actually thanked?

To thank them means deconstructing your life and asking questions like "Why do I love Chinese food?" and "Who were those guys who saved my butt that time when I locked the keys in the car downtown during rush hour?" Our lives are woven around countless other lives, whether through lifelong ties or one chance meeting. A Broadway show can leave a lasting impression on us; so can a sympathy note. All these things added together equal an unbroken life.

The process of looking at your life in this way makes you feel a little like George Bailey in *It's a Wonderful Life*, except in reverse. You're looking not for all the ways you've touched others' lives but for the way others have touched yours.

All the things in our lives that we are grateful for can be traced to someone we are grateful to. If our lives were signed, like works of art, whose signatures would be on them?

Well, this is what I thought about during that long weekend. If I knew I wasn't going to be around much longer, who would I write thank-you notes to?

Monday came, and I went for my mammogram.

The radiology resident on duty came out himself to tell me the good news: I was fine. False alarm. All clear.

But, I decided, why wait for good-byes to let everyone know how grateful I am to them? Hellos are so much happier. Why not write my thank-you notes anyway?

Most of them are already way overdue.

*"And still they lead me back
to the long, winding road . . ."*
—THE BEATLES

Dear Miss Treffery,

I would be surprised if you remembered me—or even my name—because if you've stayed in teaching these past thirty-five years, you've probably known more than a thousand students. Even if you haven't, our lives intersected such a long time ago that surely the statute of limitations for recalling long-promoted former first graders has run out.

I'm forty-one now.

My class was your first batch of students ever, I think you told my parents at Open House at the Martha W. Hoyt School, in Stamford, Connecticut. The reason I remember this is that I collected information about you as a person, not a teacher, that year, tucking it in my mind's cubbyhole to consider all evidence that you'd had a life before you came to teach at Hoyt and when you went home at night, too.

Knowing anything about our teachers outside of school in the early '60s felt like knowing secrets. It was a big thrill when the first-quarter report cards were sent home every year and a great mystery was revealed at last: your teacher's first name. You signed your name to my report card in very neat, small handwriting with loops: *Patricia Ann Treffery.*

My friends with kids tell me that now things are different. The class knows its teacher's first name even before the school year starts. Some kids even *call* their teachers by their first names. I can't imagine.

I also knew that you were from Hingham, Massachusetts, because my dad asked you that time at Open House. I treasured knowing this very personal detail about you so much that not only have I never forgotten it, but I actually asked a man I was dating in 1985, who had grown up in Hingham, if he'd known your family. He hadn't, and as things turned out with him, you were better off for it.

You weren't married—and there was no guesswork about that, because "Ms." was still ten years away—but marital status wasn't interesting to us then. A teacher was either married or would be someday, much as we'd be. Big deal. If I'd known then how infinitely complicated finding a mate is, I'd have paid more attention to how my teachers were doing in that department.

I remember all these things about you, and others, like your black hair coiffed the way some political women in Washington wear theirs, and the way you held up the chalk in your right hand, poised to write out on the blackboard the numbers we were forming on our ivory-colored plastic abacuses by sliding the jewel-colored beads up and down in columns of tens. For me, that was the start of a lifetime of being bad in math.

So I'm writing to thank you, instead, for teaching me to read.

You did this by writing a word on the blackboard—Hoyt's blackboards really were black, not green—in big capital letters with white chalk. I remember looking at the word with interest, knowing that it was a word, because you said so, and wondering how to know or guess what it was. You wouldn't give the secret away but told our class that if we just kept looking at it, you would help us read it, and afterward we would know how to go about reading any other written words we saw. (You didn't get technical about print versus script.)

We had already learned the sounds that each letter meant, and you told us to look at the chalked word and make the sounds of the letters in the order you'd written them. So I looked and made the sounds: *lllll ooooo kkkkk.* Loke? LOOK! The word was LOOK!

I will never forget the moment I knew the word was LOOK. It was the moment I went from not knowing how to read to knowing how to read. The understanding went through my brain—my whole body—like electricity.

Later, when I read *My Story,* by Helen Keller, I knew just how she felt when Annie Sullivan spelled WATER into her hand. That is still one of the best books I have ever read.

A lot has happened since I learned to read. I guess the main thing has been loving reading and stories so much that I grew up to be a book reviewer and writer. I've been "looking" at things ever since you taught me how and trying to make sense of them. I have better luck with some things than others.

My life has been full of words—those read and those written. Also—maybe because you had us read that first word out loud—words spoken. I've spent quite a few years as a speechwriter, primarily for people who were excellent in math.

Anyway, I wanted to write and thank you for showing me how to match the sounds and the symbols that break the secret code of reading. My apartment here in Washington is filled with books, some I've loved since the time I knew you, like *The Bobbsey Twins of Lakeport* and *The Five Little Peppers and How They Grew,* and others that the publishers send me to review that are not even in bookstores yet. I am grateful to you every day, because the days are adding up to a life—and a living—built on the pleasure of reading and writing.

The evolution of abacuses to calculators means I can also balance my checkbook.

Thank you for teaching me how to read.

Sincerely,

The girl with bangs and pink glasses who sat in the front row to the right of your desk.

Dear Mrs. Sullivan,

Even though you died when all the kids on the street were young, we remember you as "Wendy" instead of "Mrs. Sullivan," because when our parents talked about you, that's what they called you.

Most of us didn't know until we were teenagers that you had committed suicide.

The reason we didn't know this was that all the parents on Alma Rock Road—a cul-de-sac off a main road that could enclose secrets—conferred the day you died and decided the truth was too frightening for us. Partly they didn't want us to grow up too fast. And partly, like you, they were all in their early thirties, with young children, and your death was incomprehensible to them. So the fiction that you'd had a heart attack went on for years. It probably began when the ambulance arrived and my father, who had been a journalist, heard the police scanner blare *"Suicide"* and realized what could happen if that information got into the *Stamford Advocate*. I've never had the heart to search for your obit on microfilm, but I've been told the *Advocate* listed the cause of death as "an illness."

I still remember waking up for school that morning—it was February 1 and freezing—and hearing the phone ring in my parents' bedroom next to mine while I was still in bed. My father answered it after one ring, said, *"What?! I'll be right over!"* and ran past my room. I heard him pound down the stairs, and I knew something was very wrong; I'd never seen my father run before. I don't know what he told my mother, whether she'd known as she made us breakfast, but she told us then that Mr. Sullivan had called because you were sick.

When we came home from school that day, my father was still there and said, "Kids, we have something to tell you."

The day our parents went to your funeral, I remember sitting in school, feeling very alive, too alive, knowing you were dead. You were in fact the first person I'd known well who was dead. There are others now, including my father and other neighbors who kept the secret.

Somehow I know you know what happened afterward, how your children, Tracey and Kenny, became honorary members of our family and called my parents "Aunt Lucille" and "Uncle Howard" pretty much from that day on.

Your husband's mother and aunt came from far away Sioux Falls, South Dakota, to raise them too. Your death brought Alma Rock Road's fifteen families together, not just as neighbors but as one family, for most of my life until the first families moved out and new families moved in who didn't know you or the story.

(As it turned it, it was one of the old families who told their kids first, when they became teenagers. It didn't take long for them to spread the word and the rest of the parents to finally confirm it. I guess they figured it was time.)

Today there is all this blather about an old African proverb about its taking a village to raise a child, but in 1965, all it took was a street to raise the forty-three children who lived on it.

I could thank you for your wonderful daughter, whose busy life in Northern California as a lawyer and mom I admire and whose lifelong friendship I cherish. But there's actually something else that I've always meant to thank you for.

Sometimes in the winter, when it was too cold to walk down the street's long hill and wait for the bus, the parents would take turns driving and waiting with us in the warm car. Your black Volkswagen Beetle was a favorite, because you liked a certain radio station with good music, even though Tracey, my sister Caroline, and I would be talking and laughing and not really listening to it.

The February before you died—a year to the week— you drove us to the bus stop in the black bug, and we waited, you listening to WABC and us fooling around.

But then you turned around and said, "Now, I want you kids to be quiet and listen to this next song, because it's going to be very important, and so will the boys who are singing it."

The song was "I Wanna Hold Your Hand."

It's not hard to picture you listening to it all over again, because Tracey looks so much like you now, with the same reddish brown curly hair, pale skin and freckles. You were bundled into a dark pea coat and leaning against your door, keeping time by tapping your ungloved fingers on the bug's steering wheel. A cold rain began to fall, and you turned the windshield wipers on.

It's easy to wonder, as I sometimes do when I hear the song played on a car radio today, whether that snug bug that was warm and safe to us felt like a bell jar to you. And whether you knew the music was important not because it was fast and new but because it was restless and edgy. Like you?

Or maybe you just loved it because it sounded great, and the two moments in your life, only a year apart, that became defining moments in mine weren't related at all.

Anyway, thank you for introducing me to the Beatles.

Sincerely,

Pamela from next door

Dear Daddy,

Oh, how I wish I could thank you for letting me stay
up to watch Tiny Tim's wedding to Miss Vicki on *The
Tonight Show*. Except you didn't. Your exact words, as I
recall, were "You can stay up for the divorce."

That incident pretty much summed up our nineteen-
year relationship: damn funny at times, but with no
question about who made the rules at 54 Alma Rock Road.
In the words of the day, you wore the pants in the
family—especially when I wore bell-bottoms in junior high.
Other people might allow themselves to be governed by
their children, but there'd be no "tot-acracy," as you called
it, in *this* house.

Despite your ferocity on the subject of who was head of
household, I thought you were so funny that you should
run for president, and told you so once when you were
giving us a breakfast grammar lesson from the copy on the
back of a Lucky Charms cereal box. Now, of course, I
realize that the country could never weather a president
who remarked, "The masses are asses," every time he saw
a man-on-the-street TV news interview. You would never
have been politically correct, but I bet you would have
come up with the phrase "politically correct."

I have so much to thank you for teaching me—sharing
with me actually, because the things you taught me were
the things you yourself loved. Grammar. Words. Wordplay.
How to put words together to make your mind draw a
silly picture or say a phrase to mean something completely
different. To this day I can't start a car without thinking,
And we're off like a herd of turtles, or halt at a red light

without this in my head: *He stopped short with a bunch of jerks.*

I have so many great Howard K. Janis lines in my head. On actions and consequences: "You've buttered your bed; now lie in it." On death: "Where there's a will, there's a relative." On the endless succession of weekend gatherings at the New York relatives' homes when you tailored the Greyhound bus slogan to fit you: "Call Schmuckhound, and leave the driving to us." On eating in the car: "I am not running a dining car for mice." All four of your children still turn into Señor Wences the way you did around anything that has a lid: "S'awright."

Funny that, at forty-one, my mind leaps to words and wit when I think about what I'm grateful to you for. Not that your stubbornness, temper and sarcasm didn't make my life miserable at times. As a teenager, I wished you understood what it was like to be a girl—a girl who was definitely off like a herd of turtles on the track toward womanhood.

But we'd had something major in common since I was eight: a love of newspapers. You taught me what a lead story was one Saturday morning when just we two were on the way to Daitch Shopwell. We stopped at the High Ridge Variety Store to pick up the *Times*. You asked me to read it aloud as you drove our mud-brown Dodge Dart station wagon, the one that never quite recovered from the broken-glass-milk-bottle-in-the-back episode and forever afterward smelled like a baby on solid foods badly in need of a change.

"Look at the big headline on the top of the right side," you said. "The one in boldface—darker print. That's the story to read first."

I thought I was quite lucky and sophisticated to have all this inside information without having studied at Columbia Journalism School with a professor named Dick Baker, as you had. I feel even luckier now that I am on the inside. I'd thank you for "turning me on" to print journalism, but you hated slang, jargon and what you called "lazy writing." So thank you, instead, for conveying your love of newspapers to me, as well as your insistence on precision in spoken, as well as written, language. You were constantly telling us to both "be good" and "be careful," and though you gave those admonishments broader meaning, I've always taken them to heart when writing.

You were so gifted at calling my attention to examples of clever language in a way that made it easy to see why words were fun: the score of *My Fair Lady*, for example. Or that classic of Jewish humor, Allan Sherman's record *My Son, the Folk Singer*. Thank you for developing my love of both musical comedy and parody.

Something else you passed along that I'm unbelievably grateful for: knowing how to take rejection. This, too, started as a music lesson, from Harry Belafonte, who sang about picking yourself up, dusting yourself off, and starting all over again.

Because you liked that song so much, I really thought about the words. I didn't dream at the time that I'd come to make them a habit, but then, I didn't dream at the time that I'd come to be a writer like you. If you remember, I wanted to be an actress. Naturally, you rearranged a few words, and I became your version of the great French actress Sarah Bernhardt—Sarah Heartburn.

*   *   *

The idea that you had a pre-Daddy life fascinated me. I looked through your Kenyon College Class of 1949 yearbook constantly during my centuries-long eigthth-grade year for its clues. I think Mom always thought I had the yearbook out to gaze at your classmate Paul Newman's picture, but if she did, she was wrong (okay, sometimes, especially after I first saw *Exodus*). I felt like I hardly knew you that year; maybe knowing more about your Pre-Daddy Era would help me know you better. You were definitely of the old parenting school: "Children should be seen and not heard," you said. When it came to parents, you thought they should be both seen and heard, but only on matters relating to the proper raising of children.

When you were at work, I studied the yearbook in the room you had built on to the house the previous year. It was your study, and you issued a house rule: No Kids Allowed Unless Expressly Invited In by Daddy. Naturally, I obeyed the sanctum sanctorum dictum when you were home. Naturally, I ensconced myself on its cushy brown fake-leather couch when you weren't. This is how I discovered the *Columbia Journalism Review,* the *Foreign Affairs Quarterly, National Geographic,* Vicki Carr on eight-track, *The History of Civilization* by Will and Ariel Durant, and eventually your collection of Edgar Cayce books—which, in view of everything else I thought I knew about you, surprised the hell out of me. I bet if you were alive today, you'd read *The Celestine Prophecy.* I'd love to know what you'd think of it.

Your yearbook picture as editor of Kenyon's newspaper, *The Collegian,* shows a tall, dark, and handsome young man, a man who looked like me, seriously studying a newspaper page layout. I knew the look: you wore the exact same one when you read *The New York Times* in your study before and after dinner. Your face wore a different look when you read *The Stamford Advocate*. Boy, would I pay good money to watch you read *USA Today*. Although you might surprise me on that score: you were unexpectedly progressive when it came to journalism, reminding me often that women were journalists too. What would you think of today's EEOC guidelines, discrimination suits, and sexual harassment, I wonder.

That's what I really miss about you—the conversations we never got to have about ideas and issues, life, death and taxes. You left my life when we were still arguing about what time I had to be home, or whether you'd let me go somewhere at all. "Grow up," you'd say. "Life is hard." I told my friends you were unfair; you told me I was "immature." Even worse, you pronounced it "imma-toor."

Once a year, around Christmas, we drove to New York City to go to a party at the Narita Japanese restaurant, near Times Square. This was a very serious trip; you didn't say, "Call Schmuckhound and leave the driving to us." Caroline, Michele, and I were all decked out in velvet and bows from Mom's dress-the-girls-alike sewing phase; Gordon was costumed in his navy blue sailor suit. This Christmas party, Mom told us, was very special and important to Daddy, because he had known the man who owned the restaurant when they both had lived in Tokyo during the Korean War. The other men at the party had lived at the Overseas Press Club with Daddy in Tokyo too.

When I was old enough to understand the story behind this party, I was touched: Kami San, the restaurant's owner, had been the Tokyo OPC's houseboy during the war, and the correspondents there helped him immigrate to New York and open his restaurant afterward. The annual party was his continued thank you and honor to all of you. It's also the reason I first liked sushi when the only way I could make sense of it was by thinking of it as different kinds of lox.

It was an intriguing notion to a kid—that one's dad had had a life of adventure and travel and mystery way before he'd gone to Temple Sinai Religious School committee meetings and mowed the lawn on Saturday mornings in his undershirt and khaki trousers, a life when he'd spoken a foreign language and eaten with chopsticks.

What a wonderful gift you gave me by taking us to Kami San's parties! I don't mean just for the early exposure to things Japanese, although I thank you for that—what a window to the world for a child—but for sharing a part of your life that was special to you in ways we could only guess.

Thank you, too, for showing me that enduring ties to people you meet at certain times in your life can enrich it for all time.

Thank you especially for impressing upon me that worldliness isn't about money (I know you didn't have a lot, and it all went to supporting your family); it's about learning. And that what's important in life are not the people you know but the people who have helped you grow.

My sophomore year at Smith, when I informed you and Mom that I wanted to transfer to UCLA, the two of you drove up to Northampton on a weekday to convince me that I was being imma-toor. You were wearing a three-piece beige corduroy suit and smoking your cherrywood pipe, looking the way I'd imagined my English professors would look, before I actually got there and found them wearing turtlenecks and khakis. Mom tried to pretend she was Pat Nixon, up for the day to beg Julie to listen to her father. We went to the Wiggins Tavern, all three of us acting like WASPs, and tried to have a controlled, reasoned discussion about my leaving Smith, which was hard, because you wanted to kill me.

I was as determined to leave as you were to make me stay. Finally you said, "Kenyon is the only *possible* alternative I'll consider." Lucky for me they were admitting women by then.

So I was at Kenyon, your school, the school I loved at first sight, when Mom called six weeks later at 5 A.M. on March 6, 1976, and said simply, "Daddy's gone."

Funny, huh?

The *Stamford Advocate* covered your funeral at Temple Sinai as a news story, not an obit, because 800 people came. That was in the lead, but even so, you would have preferred the classier *New York Times* notice.

Almost from the moment you died, it seemed as though you and Edgar Cayce got together up there to guide the rest of my life. I've come not to believe in coincidences—everything happens for a reason—because here's what's happened since:

I wasn't *The Collegian's* first woman editor—that slot went to a journalist far more talented than I named Vicki Barker, one of my best friends for twenty-two years and counting. But I did work on the paper my junior year before I went back to Smith. And by the time I went back, I was ready to. Go figure.

When I went to Columbia's journalism school, your old professor, Dick Baker, was my thesis adviser.

I jumped to corporate communications after working for a daily newspaper, just as you had. And when I went to Burbank to meet an executive at Disney who interviewed me, he read my resume and said, "Are you Howard Janis's daughter?" He'd worked with you at IBM's *THINK* magazine in the '60s.

I love sushi and mysticism.

When I interviewed Paul Newman in 1997 for a *USA Weekend* story, he remembered you as "one of the good guys."

Thanks for watching over me.

How could we not know you're there? About four weeks after you died, Mom started having car trouble. When her mechanic popped the hood, he found two things: food and evidence of rodents. We'd been vermin-free the fourteen years we'd lived in that house; now suddenly we had visitors, visitors who were storing snacks from the garage trash cans in the front end of the mud-brown Plymouth Duster.

It really *was* a dining car for mice.

When journalists pass into the Fifth Estate, their footprints remain in the bylines and photos that history's heirs catalogue.

You've shown up in the darnedest places: a black-and-white ad for an electronics trade magazine you wrote for in the late '50s; a box in the University of Maryland's archives filled with Korean War memorabilia that my friend Larry

Jolidon was rooting through for his book on Korean War MIAs.

When I think about the great distances between us when you were alive, it makes me sad that we exhausted so much time and self-righteousness, me on writing my young life, you on editing it. But when I look at our relationship from the span of forty-one years and not nineteen, I see closeness. My memories are filled with our differences, but my life is crammed with our similarities.

I've come to see that closeness and the love that creates closeness are ultimately what outlive and outshine a relationship's distances and disappointments. You were right; life is hard. But it's also magical, like a story that finally makes sense when your reporting turns up the big picture. Until then, as Professor Baker used to tell both of us, you can only go with what you've got.

One of my most treasured possessions is the gold Cross pen you gave me the night of my high school senior-class awards. The English department gave me the writing award that night, but that pen, your personal award for my writing, meant more to me. Thanks for being my first and best journalism teacher—and my father.

Love,

Your daughter Pamela

P.S.: You were right about Tiny Tim's getting divorced. He was divorced several times, in fact. When he died last year, I couldn't help but smile, remembering.

Dear Cousins Loretta and Izzy,

You gave me a peak experience by making me the flower girl at your wedding when I was five. Do I remember it? Are you *kidding*?!

Thank you for the first experience in my life that I remember as "thrilling." The excitement began even before the actual wedding night with The Shopping for the Shoes. For some reason, although I loved my light pink organdy dress with the ruffles and the ribbon sash tied in a bow in back, it was those white patent leather Mary Janes, my first "big girl" pair, that I went wild over. (Cousin Loretta's big-girl shoes were probably killing her that night, but your flower girl couldn't have been more blissed out if she'd been wearing glass slippers like Cinderella's.)

So there were the shoes. And the big hotel in New York where Aunt Harriet told me all the ladies had to go to the ladies' room before the bride could come out. (To this day I arrive at hotels, synagogues, churches, wherever, for weddings—and head for the ladies' room like Pavlov's niece.) And the food and the music and the ladies' beautiful gowns and the men's black and white special suits. (My father hated tuxes the way he hated opera, with the concession that once in a while you'd be invited and just have to do it.)

And the bride . . . Wow, the bride! Loretta, you were the first real, live bride I ever saw. Is there any way to describe how beautiful you were to me besides admitting that I dressed as a bride one Halloween soon thereafter? (So I haven't *always* been a bridesmaid.) Ask my mother how many times the only thing that would keep me occupied when I was sick was Bride & Groom cut-outs.

(Appalling cultural conditioning in retrospect, but I loved them.) I'm afraid Izzy didn't fare well in the continuing Wedding-as-Fantasy, Bride-as-Fantastic-Creature department; those cardboard guys and black tuxes were pretty uninteresting (and interchangeable) to me. But I always named the bride Loretta. Izzy, you wouldn't believe how many times your wife has been married since I was your flower girl.

It was a smashing night all the way around, including the part when Izzy stepped on the glass and broke it. Fabulous. Thank you for the ensuing lifetime of memories and unrealized hopes. Just kidding.

I loved being your flower girl and tried to scatter the soft-as-skin rose petals the right way, a little at a time. Sorry I halted the ceremony when I stopped in the aisle to pose for that man with a camera. Everyone laughed, but hey, the look of pure joy on my face in that photo is an eternal reminder for me that happiness can be as real as a *ketuba*, a Jewish wedding contract.

I have one other thing about that magical night to thank you for: it was the first time I saw midnight. And I really *saw* it—there was a big clock in the hotel ballroom, and my father had already explained about midnight to me. He and my mother wanted me to go to sleep somewhere—a hotel room, the car, I don't remember— but I wasn't about to miss Cinderella's hour, no sirree. At 11:30 P.M., my father picked me up like "It's been a big day; let's go," but I begged to be allowed to stay up to see midnight. For whatever reason, my father let me (and then clearly figured I owed him early bedtimes until I left for college). That's how I got to see midnight come and go for the very first time. I was struck, as it were, by the amazing truth that you could wait for a single, special minute for forever, it seemed, and then it was gone in that same minute.

I don't think I've gone to bed before midnight since. (This is true: my friends and clients all laugh that I live in Washington, D.C., on Pacific time. When I'm in my second "home," San Francisco, do I adjust to "normal" business and sleeping hours? No! Then I'm on Hawaiian time. It's all your fault.)

Late nights will forever hold for me the sense of anticipation, excitement and promise that your wedding night did.

I also happen to have a huge shoe collection, but I can't pin that one on you—Nordstrom came east.

Thank you for asking your cousin Lucille's eldest daughter to be the flower girl at your wedding. There have been few thrills to equal it since.

Love,

Pamela

Dear Lucille Ball and Desi Arnaz,

I don't think I realized that *I Love Lucy* was off the air by the time I was old enough to watch it. I thought you were making the show long after you'd stopped—several times a day, in fact.

Thank you for making me laugh so hard when I was growing up, especially when I was sick and stayed home from school. If I were a kid today, I wouldn't *want* to stay home from school—what, to watch Jerry Springer? Back then, sick days were great: you, *The Dick Van Dyke Show*, *Leave It to Beaver*, *The Donna Reed Show*, *Dennis the Menace*, *Make Room for Daddy*, *Andy Griffith*, *Bewitched* ("Sam? SAM!"), *I Dream of Jeannie*, *The Fugitive*, and *Queen for a Day* (a pathetic offering, in retrospect, but better than telling the world how awful your life is on one of today's talk shows and then not winning anything for it).

In my day (I sound like my mother), the unhappy grown-ups' shows were all soap operas and didn't start until 2 P.M. By that time I was bored with TV and wanted to make cut-outs instead. (My childhood illnesses weren't exactly dire.)

I never stopped loving *Lucy*. Years later, when my friend Toots in San Francisco was still single and I'd go to visit, we'd get up at 9 A.M. to watch two episodes back-to-back (the Bay Area was progressive even when it came to reruns) in our pajamas, huddling near the space heater in her apartment on Ashbury Street. Once in L.A., I made my friend Jeff Gottlieb retrace your, Ethel's, and Fred's stops there with me—"But I draw the line at the Brown Derby," he said. (We did, however, go to the Polo Lounge at the Beverly Hills Hotel, where they made jacketless Jeff put on a sport coat that they kept in a closet full of them for underdressed patrons.)

Before there was CNN, there was *I Love Lucy*. Once when I was in St. Maarten, I stepped into a garden of poison ivy (believing the local who had insisted there was no poison ivy on St. Maarten) and soon found myself in an island doctor's waiting room full of Caribbean, French, Dutch, Japanese and Mexican tourists, all of us watching his TV while we waited. There was Lucy, getting stuck in the wet cement at Graumann's Chinese Theatre for the 957th time in my life while an international roomful of sick people laughed in one language as if they'd seen this before under similar circumstances.

Is that what the whole world did when it stayed home from school, watch *Lucy*?

I never went in for the *Lucy* backlash: "It's sexist"; "Look how he tries to dominate her"; "Look how she plays games and tricks him." Yeah, yeah, yeah. I went to Smith, school of Gloria and Betty; I *know*. I worry about Barbie's impact on developing female minds and bodies and secretly suspect that believing the words to "Some Enchanted Evening" from the score of *South Pacific* may have led to my irrational scanning of strangers' eyes across crowded rooms. Would I want to be married to Ricky Ricardo? No, thanks. Is Lucy a role model? Yeah, right up there with Jeannie. But I'll never forsake *Lucy*. It would be like boycotting *Seinfeld* because George is a schmuck, Kramer's dysfunctional, Jerry's emotionally immature, and Elaine is self-involved.

"My get-up-and-go got up and went."
"Well-done, Medium Raya."
"Splain!"

Thanks for all the funny plots, clever lines, physical comedy, elastic faces and chemistry between you that made me love *Lucy*. Thanks, too, to William Frawley and Vivian Vance, for making your gifted twosome a foursome and for making so many people the world over eternally laugh themselves sick even when they aren't already.

Sincerely,

Pamela Janis

Dear Otto,

If you are alive today, you must be ancient, because the Hoyt and Northeast Elementary kids on your school bus thought you were very old even back then.

What were you, thirty-five?

I'm one of those kids.

I wanted to thank you for your careful driving and for being on time even when I wasn't.

Also, do you remember that you were making the afternoon run the day President Kennedy was assassinated? I do. I was in second grade. I was sitting right behind you when the bus stopped at Martha Purdy's stop and the parents who were there told you the news they'd just heard. I couldn't hear what they'd said to you, but I saw your head and back shake. You sat for a long time without starting up the bus again. Everyone got quiet; we must have sensed something was wrong. Then you turned around and told us:

"Our President Kennedy's been shot dead."

At first we were shocked, because we'd never seen a man cry before, Negro or not. Then we were frightened that President Kennedy was so suddenly dead. But only you knew what the news meant. We were too young to see into the future, but you were so very old you could.

You started up the bus, and I watched your tears find their way around your ears and into the creases of the back of your thick neck and trickle down, down, until they disappeared under your shirt collar. Nobody said another word the whole rest of that ride. We didn't even say " 'Bye" to you, and you didn't say " 'Bah" to us like always. And everyone's parents were at their bus stops.

I've never forgotten you or that day or how sad you were, driving your school bus, on it, and I wanted to tell you thanks for delivering us home safely and on time always, but especially on November 22, 1963.

> Sincerely,
>
> *The little girl at High Ridge and Alma Rock Road who had the black Barbie lunch box.*

Dear Gordon,

The thrilling words "You have a baby brother" came
first from Mrs. Stumpe, Kathy's mother; she'd come
upstairs to Kathy's bedroom to deliver the news after
Grandma Ida called. I think we were redecorating Kathy's
dollhouse at the time—it's a measure of my wonder at
your birth that I can't remember precisely what we were
doing even though it's only been thirty-four years.

You'd remember a detail like that. In my whole life (and
yours), I've never met anyone who remembers details the
way you do. I'd swear you actually *read* the Almanac. You
are also quite amazing at recognizing faces—a fact that I'm
sure John Anderson, the only presidential candidate to
look, as you say, like Dennis the Menace's father,
appreciated when you said hello to him buying shirts in
Hecht's that time. Or was it Woodies? I'm sure you
remember.

"C'mon," Mrs. Stumpe said. "I'll drive you home."

Kathy didn't see what the big deal was; she had *two*
brothers. But I knew I had to go home. It makes me laugh
now to think about it—you, Mom and Daddy were an
hour away in New York. (Mom delivered only at Mount
Sinai Hospital the way some women shopped only at
Bergdorf's.) Why did I have to go home? This is such a
peculiarly Jewish reaction to big news, good or bad,
whether something happens in your family or in Israel:
You go home. Not only do you go home, but you go home
with the feeling that when you get there, you're going to
huddle around the radio with your family, awaiting further
tragic news from Pearl Harbor.

This, by the way, is why I loved opera when I

discovered it: every production is like a typical day in the life of a Jewish family. Drama! Comedy! Angst! Elation! Complicated relationships! Ulterior motives! Misunderstandings! Ahas! Estrangement! Reconciliation! Banishment! Reunions! Sobbing! Laughter! Deaths! Births!

So you see, I do not digress after all.

I went home at the news of your birth to huddle around the kitchen wall phone with Caroline, Michele and Grandma Ida awaiting further joyous news from Mount Sinai.

A baby brother! Wow!

I have to tell you, I've never gotten over the fact that you exist. "I mean that in a good way." (I never know who I'm quoting anymore, you or Seinfeld.)

One day, October 15, 1964, we were a family of just girls—Daddy didn't count, although for some reason Mom did—and the next day we were complete.

So the first thing I want to thank you for is for being born. Roughly 2,491,017 people have asked me during my lifetime about my family, three of them at job interviews, the rest of them on dates, and my answer still fills me with pride: "I have two sisters and . . . [meaningful pause] a brother."

Of course, there are many meanings contained in that statement, but for you I'll elaborate.

Having a brother, when you're a little girl, is having a passport to a different cultural world. Maybe I should amend that to "when you're a little girl in a rabidly gender-specific family in the '60s." Until you arrived, the house in Stamford was a dollhouse, with my Barbie and Chatty Cathy, Caroline's Kissy and Michele's Raggedy Ann. No wonder we treated you like another one. But your world had Matchbox cars, a train set and your beloved baseball cards.

Having a brother, when you're a teenage girl, is initially a reason to believe that not all boys are creepy, mean or gross. Later, it's a reason to believe that one of them might like you too.

Having a brother, when you're a woman, is having a male friend who can always provide the Male Perspective to explain the apparently inexplicable behavior of other males. More than that, it is having a totally different and unique view of things dear to you: family matters and relationships, social and political ideas, your own cultural heritage.

I've always been glad I have a brother for all those reasons. But having *you* as a brother—now, that's what I'm truly grateful for.

Your loyalty is uniquely you. (Especially to me. No matter how busy I get or how many days or weeks go by in a work blur, I know I can count on hearing from you on my answering machine: "Just calling to check in.") You are just so good at glueing the family together when we're all busy doing our own things.

You are such a *guttinke*. I can't tell you how much I appreciate your willingness to just be *available* to family and friends who might be in need . . . your unfailing "Can I bring you anything?" in times of sickness or stress. "You know," you said to me that time Callie turned into Attack Cat, sending me to the emergency room with puncture wounds from her little fangs—she's never as forbearing as you during my busy weeks—"you should have called me."

"It was late, you were probably asleep, I couldn't stop

to pick you up, it was faster just to get there. . . . Yadda, yadda, yadda."

"You should have woken me up," you insisted. "I could have taken a taxi. *You should have called me*."

Speaking of which, thanks for feeding Callie when I've been away. Thanks, too, for driving us both to the airport that time I took her to California with me, breaking speed records on 95 North to get us there on time. When we arrived—on time—you said, "No problem." Thanks for saying that, even though I can't believe having a nervous passenger plunging a tranquilizer-loaded pill gun down an animal's throat in the backseat of a Geo isn't a problem.

For your willingness to always do not just the right thing but the *extra* thing; for your continuing courage during times of uncertainty; for never missing a pop-culture reference from the past four decades; for all these things, I admire you and thank you. You may have been the last member of Howard and Lucille's family to make the scene, but you're definitely its biggest booster, not to mention its most authoritative baseball source.

Thanks for being, first, as Mrs. Stumpe announced you, my "baby brother." Thanks even more for being my brother now.

Love,

*P*am

Dear Mattel,

I was a "You-can-tell-it's-Mattel-it's-swell" girl back
when Barbie's hair hadn't yet grown down to her in-line
skates and her friends were named Midge and cousin
Francie, not Barbie, Barbie and Barbie. I swear, I don't
recall a single Northeast Elementary schooler who had
more than one Barbie. How can you play with a group of
dolls who have the same name unless you pretend they're
sextuplets and give them all different middle names? But
even then they all have the same hair, more or less, so
where's the fun in that?

My own "fashion" Barbie (do you still call her that?)
had a titian pageboy. I remember the hair color name
stamped on the box was "titian" because once when we
were nine, Kathy Stumpe was over, with her blonde
ponytailed Barbie, and I said, God knows why, "I *hate* red
hair."

Kathy got quiet and looked hurt. "Even mine?" she
asked.

I looked at her, sized up the situation and said
disdainfully, "I *meant* titian."

That was my first acquaintance with the concept of
damage control. Hard to believe I didn't grow up to be a
White House press secretary, isn't it?

So if everyone has a Daryl Hannah–in–*Splash*–looking
Barbie these days, how are you supposed to learn about
putting a cork in it? Kids today . . . Oh, never mind. I'm
not writing you about Barbie anyway. I *meant* to thank you
for Chatty Cathy.

Now, she was a *doll*.

I adored Chatty Cathy because my father said she looked just like me. (Give me a break; I was five.) In fact, he saw her first, out shopping with my mother, before I ever knew she existed. The story, as my mom tells it, is that my dad bought her on the spot because he wanted to watch my face when I looked at hers.

Chatty Cathy and I both had below-shoulder-length—but not long—dark brown hair, brown eyes under long lashes, a stub nose and a slight overbite. I fell in love with her instantly.

I was enchanted that she talked. I pulled the string that led to her internal torso voice box by its orangey thin plastic ring over and over again to hear her say, "I'm hungry" . . . "I'm tired" . . . "What's *your* name?"

Then tragedy struck: I drew out Chatty Cathy's string . . . and it broke.

My father called your company right away.

He and my mother told me that the doll hospital in California where Chatty Cathy was born could do an operation on her and make her all better. But, they said, California was very far away from Oceanside, New York, my first home, so Chatty Cathy might be there for a long time, a few weeks, even.

I dressed her very tenderly for the trip.

Three weeks later, the doorbell rang one afternoon, and there was a man with Chatty Cathy in a box. (Thank you, UPS.)

My fingers were shaking in excitement; my mother had to cut the string with the big-girl scissors. There she was, lying as I'd dressed her for the journey, her eyes closed, their long lashes resting on her little molded cheeks. She looked like an angel without wings.

I lifted her carefully out of the box, and she opened her brown eyes to me. Oh!

Gently I pulled the operated-on string. Chatty Cathy said, "I'm hungry."

"Well, of course you are," I told her lovingly. "You just came all the way from California."

Thank you for making Chatty Cathy all better that time.

Unfortunately, my relationship with my dad seemed to get worse over the ensuing years. It seemed like we were always mad at each other. I must have gotten mad at Chatty Cathy, too, because I lost her somewhere along the way to Barbie.

Years later, in West Virginia with my then-boyfriend Phil, I couldn't believe my eyes. There she was in the back of an antique store. Oh!

Chatty Cathy was sitting on a shelf, dressed in a sleeveless grayish pink sateen nightgown edged with torn cream-colored lace. She'd been a haircut victim; I empathized with her. Her face was dirty. Her string was broken. But her eyes under their long lashes looked into mine and pleaded, "I need a mommy."

She was $35, considerably more than my father had paid for her in 1961.

"I have to have her," I told Phil. "She's my inner child."

He nodded in understanding, then reached for a Yankee Stadium photograph of his inner team.

Thank you, Mattel, for Chatty Cathy. For both Chatty

Cathys, really: the first one that a father brought home to delight his little girl when their relationship was never more perfect, and the second to remind her of when it was.

Sincerely,

Pamela Janis

P.S.: Thanks for the Barbie I loved too.

Dear Miss Riordan,

If you ever made the consciousness-raised move to "Ms." Riordan, I never heard about it. To me you will always be "Miss Riordan," because during your long administrative career at both Hoyt and Northeast Elementary schools, every teacher and grade schooler in town knew you as *Miss*. Such was your power that even *parents* called you Miss Riordan. Stamford's little girls were still calling you Miss Riordan at Linney Preis's wedding twenty years after they'd been sent to your office for the last time.

Did you know we—even the boys—all were afraid of you? I bet yours were the only schools in the country where it was scarier to get sent to the assistant principal than to the principal. There was something gentle and romantic about the principal, Mr. Carlucci—all the girls thought he was handsome, like their fathers—but, oh boy, you were another story. At your full height—of, what, five feet one, including your coiffed hair and your click-click-click high heels—with just a look, you could make any second-grade boy who threw one of those pink arrow-shaped, pencil-top erasers across a classroom regret it into his fifth decade. Or the girls who, no matter how many times the teacher warned them, just couldn't seem to stop giggling with their neighbor.

I couldn't help it. Kathy Stumpe was making me laugh.

She grew up to write sitcoms, by the way. But that's another story.

School discipline in the '60s meant that nobody "acted out"; they were "bad." I just can't picture you ever saying anything '90s like "It's not *you* I don't love; it's the Fruit

Stripes gum you're chewing." Or "Good job!" to the aspiring Wilt Chamberlains who happened to score a wastebasket from their seats. Young ladies and gentlemen in your schools *walked* to the wastebaskets, or they walked to your office. And it wasn't called a time-out when they did.

I've never seen anything like your "I-will-not-tolerate-such-conduct" stare since, and believe me, some local politicians, police chiefs and dubious achievers that I've reported on have tried their best on me. If you think I sassed you that time in your office when you asked if I understood how precarious my mortal state was at that moment (I understood subtext at an early age) and I said, "Yes," instead of "Yes, Miss Riordan," you should hear my answer to anyone who asks, "Did you have to put *that* in the newspaper?"

Now, my guess is that you will be surprised to hear that I was afraid of you, because we were always sort of special friends. Do you remember?

In second grade when we learned about weaving, I wove you that green-and-white . . . thing . . . and shyly and nervously gave it to you as a present. And you kept it on the second grader–sized captain's chair in your office for years—the one bad kids sat in—at least until I went to junior high school (I hope even longer). And I always liked you and was never afraid of you after that, because I realized you were *nice*.

Why did I do that? I wonder.

It took years to figure this one out, but here's what I learned from you: When you make friends with what you're afraid of, you're not afraid of it anymore.

Thank you for this school-of-life teaching.

You can't know how well it has served me: from professors to bosses; flying to public speaking; illnesses to deaths; rejection, disappointment and loss; you name it—whatever I've been afraid of has ceased to terrify me once I made its acquaintance. And I have you to thank for discovering this.

I was so happy to see you at Linney's wedding that I hugged you, even though by then I think I had a good six inches on you in my click-click-click high heels. Or does what's fearful just look smaller when you embrace it?

Yes, Miss Riordan.

Love,

Your former Hoyt/Northeaster

Dear Sidney Poitier,

To Sir, With Love has always been one of my favorite movies, and for thirty-two years I've wanted to thank you for it.

I heard the dramatic ba-*boom* of the opening drum for the first time when I was nine, sitting in the State Theatre in Springdale with a girl from my street. She was a year or two older than me, with enviably smooth hair. She was very sophisticated. I smoked my first cigarette with her a few years later, feeling like one of the girls in your movie classroom—bad, but only because I was misunderstood, had exasperating parents, and my talents were as yet untapped by a gorgeous male teacher determined to reach me as no one else could. Naturally, it was Pamela Dare I identified with, the girl you called by name instead of "Miss Dare" the day of the school dance. When you looked into her eyes and said meaningfully, "Pamela," I imagined it was me you were saying it to.

How sophisticated, elegant, and dignified you were as Sir! I had such a crush on you. Trying to choose between you and Paul McCartney, had it come to that (and in the pre–junior high girl world—where no one had a bustline, ergo anything still seemed possible—I believed it could) was like trying to choose between Rocky Road and Strawberry Cheesecake at Baskin-Robbins. I used to tell myself I had at least an equal chance of marrying either one of you.

When To Sir went to Channel 7's 4:30 movie—the late '60s version of going to video—I made sure I was home after school the days it ran, I don't know how many times. I memorized whole paragraphs of dialogue, punctuation included: " . . . *Those kids are devils incarnate! I have tried everything . . . but nothing I have tried . . .*"

I played the 45 over and over, too; I'm probably the only human being in the world besides Lulu the singer's mother who remembers that the flip side was something called "The Boat That I Row."

What I especially loved about you in *To Sir* was the way you wove stoicism, hopefulness, compassion and pain into your acting. To me, you *were* Sir. Even when I read the book by E. R. Braithwaite—the real-life Sir—I could not imagine Sir being anyone but you, or you being anyone but Sir. I loved the book but frankly couldn't imagine E. R. Braithwaite, whoever he was, as *you.*

I've seen the movie dozens of times over the years. It has never failed to move me to tears. All I need is that first ba-*boom* to get me started. By the time the museum trip photo montage comes on, I'm a mess. The gym scene? Forget it. Getting off the bus, turning the corner and coming upon the class before Seals's mother's funeral: what are you trying to *do* to people?

When Lulu sings the theme song at the dance and the little Asian girl comes toward you with the gift box, the rest of the movie gets blurry for me. That triumphant moment of impulsive decision when, alone in the classroom after those kids run in, you rip up the letter with the job offer—was there ever a movie moment so made for cheering?

You have given the world so many lustrous, impassioned performances that it seems unfair to single Sir out from the rest of your work. Yet for me *To Sir, With Love* is the movie that catapulted me into the understanding that a great actor is one who confuses you the same way a dream does: by conjuring emotions from your own imagination's work into a sleight-of-mind consciousness.

I've thought about writing you to thank you for the movie for more than three decades. So, naturally, when I finally sat down to do it, God had to remind me that the magic of acting begins with a great story from a gifted writer. Here's what happened to me Christmas Eve, 1997, about a week after I first began this letter to you:

I got to my friend Joanne's dinner party in Virginia late; all the other guests were already there. Two friends of Joanne's, a man and a woman I didn't recognize, moved forward for introductions.

"Hello," said the man, sophisticated, elegant and dignified, with a dark suit, a pocket handkerchief smartly triangulated, and a hand extended. "I'm Ted Braithwaite."

Well, it didn't register until after the party, when Joanne informed me that I'd just spent an evening with the *real* Sir and his wife. The amazing thing was that he did, in fact, remind me of *you*. As him, I mean.

I hope you don't mind sharing this thank you with E. R. Braithwaite—Ted—for one of the most powerful, enduring and resonant stories ever to come to life for me. Or come to art—both your spells, story and acting, were so enthralling that I'm still not sure which is really which.

Thank you both for *To Sir, With Love*.

Sincerely,

Pamela (Dare) Janis

Dear Mr. Stone,

Thank you for teaching me how to swim!

How did it come about that my parents asked you, a neighbor on our street and their good friend, to give me swimming lessons? I don't know that I ever knew the story behind our after-dinner (but *always* an hour or more after) classes the summer I turned ten. But I remember walking down the street to your house at the corner of Alma Rock Road, wearing my bathing suit under my shorts, and then following you down the wooded path to the lake, the same lake that Franny Borderud had me pushing chairs across when it was frozen in February, trying to teach me to ice-skate.

Clearly, my parents weren't sports-minded themselves. If I needed a word's definition, my dad was definitely the guy to ask; my mother was the needlepoint queen. But athletics? Forget it.

Somehow—thanks, Mom—I thought this was a Jewish thing. "Jews believe in education," was the way she put it. "Jews aren't jocks." Was there a Jewish child in the country who didn't hear from his or her parents about how even The Exception, Sandy Koufax, didn't pitch on Yom Kippur? The rallying cry for every Sisterhood member trying to corral her kid in the car to get to Hebrew school on time was, "He's a Jew first, then a ballplayer."

Why I never thought to point out the obvious to my parents—that *you* were Jewish and knew how to swim—I'll never know.

But I still know everything you taught me those long summer evenings in the cool lake water: the dead man's float, the scissors kick and, finally, the crawl. I think of you whenever I go swimming.

Thank you for teaching me one of my most enjoyable pastimes (along with ice-skating).

Love,

Pamela

Dearest Franny,

I have never gotten used to the fact that you're gone, even though it's been almost twenty years since you died. It's still incomprehensible to me that you, who were so full of life, had to go.

There's been a huge void in my life ever since.

Besides making me a passionate anti-smoker, your death made me realize how one unique individual can single-handedly have an impact on someone's life for far longer than you're actually blessed with them. Just the other day, Michele described a lakeside house she and Bobby had looked at, this way: "I've always wanted to be Franny-on-the-lake."

Being able to swim in the lake behind your house, the lake you named "Lake Inferior," wasn't the only reason every child on Alma Rock Road rang your doorbell. You were a kid magnet. Something about you, even though you were our parents' age, made you seem like everyone's best friend. I certainly counted you as one of mine. Your thick black hair in its headband, deep-set brown eyes peeking from under their long mascaraed lashes, big smile and mischievous sense of humor drew people to you like small summer picnickers to your sandy patch of beach.

I'd never met such a funny woman as you, or one who seemed so interested in what I thought about everything. You may have had three sons, but you were a girl's girl for every age: directing the making of chocolate chip cookies, inviting and keeping the confidences of my agonizing adolescence, and evoking the most hilarious and most serious long-distance conversations from and about college. You were always the first person I tore off down the street to see on school breaks and the last I said good-bye to when I left. At every age, going to visit you felt like going to a party: even though I didn't know exactly what might happen, I knew I'd have fun just being there.

When I was six and first met you as "our neighbor, Mrs. Borderud," you endeared yourself to me immediately by breaking one of my parents' strict rules: Thou Shalt Call Adults "Mr. and Mrs. So-and-So." "Oh, call me Franny," you said. I dubiously asked my mother if I could; she, apparently realizing that you were magical, made the exception.

That made you my first grown-up friend. But your friends were of all ages: kids, teenagers, parents, even the dogs on the street flocked to your house. You met everyone's grandparents when they came to visit from out of town. My Grandpa Max and Grandma Helen, who otherwise felt like gefilte fish out of Bronx water when they came to "the country," as they called it, felt at home with you and would ask my mother in every phone call, "How's Frenny?"

It seemed as if you were a member of every family on the street, and every person on it was a member of yours.

Thank you for such an enriching example of friendship. I've made it a point ever since I've known you to have friends of all ages. (And species. Maybe it was just years of seeing you trailed by your dachshunds, Schaatze and Benjy, but for me a home isn't a home unless there's a creature or two joining me on the couch.)

The practical jokes began soon after we moved in. I think my father started it. You used to crack everyone up with your stories of your Italian childhood in New Jersey: "Cops always came to our family funerals to write down the license plate numbers." ("I don't get it," I'd say to my father, who was shaking with laughter. "Why did the police go to the funeral?") So my dad came up with a great joke when he went to Italy on a business trip: he wrote you a postcard saying a bunch of relatives were coming from Sicily to live with you and that they hoped you had room for the two goats. He signed it: *Your Cousin, Luigi.*

You retaliated by sending my mother a Rock Cornish game hen stuffed into the corner of an eight-foot-tall freight box, knowing she was expecting a huge turkey as a prize from that call-in radio trivia show you both listened to in the afternoon. *Fortune Phone,* I think it was called. I remember how excited my mother was when that box was delivered and how she pawed through newspaper wrappings eight feet deep before she unearthed the truncated frozen bird. "What the—?" she wondered, then grabbed a newspaper, saw it was *The Stamford Advocate,* and realized: *"Franny!"*

You and she used to have ridiculous conversations like this:

MY MOTHER: "I'm having sixteen for Thanksgiving; we're starting with kreplach."
YOU: *"Kreplach?!* What kind of appetizer is kreplach for an American holiday?"
MY MOTHER: "What are *you* having?"
YOU: "Ravioli."

What an incredibly resourceful and able woman you were. You always believed in starting with the hardest thing, the biggest challenge, in anything you undertook, because, you said, after it, everything else would be easy. When you first married Bill Borderud and had to learn how to iron, you started with one of his shirts. When you wanted to learn to sew, you started with a raincoat. Was there nothing you couldn't do? I never knew when I showed up at your house whether I'd find you antiquing furniture or layering lasagna. I wonder what you'd think of Martha Stewart—especially since you always quoted Phyllis Diller, that era's version of Roseanne.

I was always asking you for advice, especially about my parents during those interminable teen years when they shifted into only two gears: unreasonable and embarrassing.

"You want my advice?" you'd say. "Don't eat yellow snow."

Then you'd proceed to give me what I invariably thought was the best advice in the world. Because I knew if it came from you, it not only made good sense but was respectful of everyone involved, including me. All my life, you've been my model for nonjudgmental listening, for putting myself in the other person's place, and for trying to be of real help. Everyone tells you to do that, but very few people show you how by doing it themselves. You were the first person in my life who did. How do you thank someone for that?

The only thing you refused to advise me on or help me with was smoking. I think I was thirteen when I asked you to teach me how to do it. You were adamant in your refusal: "No. You're too young."

I wish now that all my memories of you didn't conjure the picture of you drawing on a Salem Menthol. That's unfair—you really enjoyed smoking, I know, and it's hard to imagine you as you without a cigarette, the open pack next to you, matchbook tucked into the cellophane. It's totally selfish for me to wish you'd quit, or assume you'd never have gotten lung cancer if you had, but do you have any idea how many people have never stopped missing you?

I was in journalism school when you died, but the end really began one afternoon the previous spring when I was working at NBC. I called you to tell you some silly story or another, and you were very quiet. Finally, you said, "Honey, I just got some bad news."

Hard to believe that the short after-school winter afternoons in your kitchen and den, the long summer days on the screened porch overlooking the sun-shimmery lake, had really ended. They and you were like love—no matter what anyone says, you really expect it to go on forever.

Somewhere in a storage box there's an audiocassette lying around of the group you dubbed "Gordon Janis & the Shrill Sisters" singing about your favorite cookies, Pecan Sandies, to the tune of "Big Girls Don't Cry." Somewhere in Mark's or Jon's or Scott's consciousness are the rest of the lyrics to your song that began, "They tried to sell us egg foo yung." Somewhere out there I know you're dancing to the score of your favorite movie, *Saturday Night Fever,* still crazy about John Travolta. And, with my dad, staging some of the cosmic jokes that seem to continually befall me.

I still have the brown stuffed dachshund you made for each of your boys to take to college in turn. Thanks for giving it to me after Scott graduated from the Naval Academy—I felt so honored.

Thank you for being my first adult friend and for teaching me how to enjoy people of all ages and kinds. The gift you had of making children feel important, like grown-ups, and grown-ups playful, like children, is, like your sense of humor, yours alone. I can never thank you enough for sharing it with me as long as you could, for being there as long as you were, for forever being not Mrs. Borderud, but Franny.

Love,

Pamela

Dear Angela Lansbury,

I'm sorry to admit that I didn't watch *Murder, She Wrote* more than a few times in all the years it was on TV. Instead, this is an overdue thank-you note for a much earlier triumph: I saw you when you were *Mame* on Broadway in 1966, and I've never forgotten it.

Mame was the very first Broadway show I ever saw. My mother took me to see it the summer after fifth grade for my eleventh birthday. I'd wanted to see the show without really knowing what it was about, because my class that year had put on a show, written by my teacher, about four people touring New York City. When they reached Broadway, where *Mame* and *Fiddler on the Roof* were then playing, Jimmy Simon sat on a roof with a violin from the music room while the chorus sang *Fiddler*. Then they sang *Mame*. I was Mame.

Being Mame meant that I had to parade back and forth on the stage during the song, wearing a long, slinky black dress (I think it was my teacher's), holding a long cigarette holder with an unlit cigarette and trying not to pitch forward in the size 4 glittery spike heels I'd borrowed from tiny Mrs. Brock, who lived on our street. From this I deduced that Mame must be a grand, glamorous character indeed and asked my parents if we could go see the real *Mame*.

I'm amazed they took me—my mother looked aghast when Miss Gooch showed up pregnant in act 2—but it was a wish granted, and I've loved *Mame* ever since.

My goodness, I'd never seen anyone as grand and glamorous as you. Or as boozy and blowsy as Bea Arthur, who played Vera. Or as prim and naive as Jane Connell, Miss Gooch.

Thirty years later, I remember the entire cast of that show, all the sets, all the songs, and the amazement I felt that you all could act, dance and sing at the same time.

No other Broadway show has satisfied me quite so much since, and I've seen all the great ones: you and *Mame* started my lifelong love of musical comedy: *Fiddler, Guys and Dolls, My Fair Lady, A Chorus Line* . . . what a marvelous gift you gave me! But *Mame* was the best of them all for me, and I wanted you to know.

As it turned out, I was to be one of those characters in our class play that "toured" Manhattan years later when I moved there after college and stayed for graduate school. I wonder if the excitement of being introduced to New York by way of *Mame* made me more of a city booster than its rents, rats, muggings, noise and traffic actually merited. But, you see, the skyline has thrilled me with the same amount of anticipation with which I first saw it unveiled in *Mame* when the curtain went up after the overture.

Life has many moments that connect present with past—moments that seem so random as to be deliberate. These are the moments that seem to "tie things together," to remind us of something important, to alert us to something we need to notice, to free us, to mark us.

One of mine came the year I left New York, when my then-boyfriend introduced me to a boarding-school friend of his, the son of Patrick Dennis, the real Mame's nephew who had written the book on which *Mame* is based. I couldn't believe it, I was so thrilled! And what of his legendary great-aunt?, I eagerly asked.

He paused.

She was alive, then in her eighties or even nineties, living in a faded nursing home in the Village. She was poor, destitute even, in shabby surroundings. The nursing home was broke; the city might have to close it. Her memory was mostly gone. There was no trace of the life that had been immortalized as larger than.

How sad that we toast characters and set aside people.

For me, that was the second-act curtain dropping on New York City's exuberance.

But *Mame* is a moment in time that's always mine to revisit, and when I do, I remember its grandeur and glamour, starring Angela Lansbury.

You gave a hell of a performance at the Winter Garden theater that day. Thanks.

Sincerely,

Pam Janis

Dear Grandma Ida and Grandpa Jack,

Any tea table that has both a sugar bowl and a dish of lemon wedges on it instantly brings to mind Grandpa Jack saying, "Please pass me my disposition." I was seven, on my first week-long sleepover at your apartment in Forest Hills, when I started reaching for the lemon with a straight face, intuitively knowing it was in the timing.

Grandpa Jack and I always had that special bond of wryness that made me giggle and him chuckle. "Look at that," he'd say, navigating the big white Buick, nodding at a sign in Chinese taped to an abandoned storefront window. "I know you can read *that*." In the backseat, I'd pretend to be making out the words, one by one: "Chinese . . . restaurant . . . opening . . . here . . . soon." He'd slap the steering wheel, chuckling, while Grandma Ida, next to him in the front seat, unexpectedly began to laugh too. Mostly she was a quiet lady, smallish, demure and gray-haired, who smoked Kent cigarettes and told stories about Daddy and Aunt Stefanie when they were growing up—leading us to believe they were perfectly behaved, polite children who never made noise or quarreled—but every once in a while she'd abruptly start chuckling as though a sally had caught her by surprise.

It wasn't until I was a teenager that I learned Grandma Ida hadn't always smoked and had gray hair or a tentative laugh. Your proper way of doing things and particular care where children's "big ears" were concerned made it inevitable that the most important family stories were as shut away in your memories as Grandma's Kents were in one of the white-painted kitchen drawers that jammed when you tried to open or close it.

Eventually, when our mother told us about the baby boy who died of meningitis when he was three, who would have been my uncle Ernest had he lived, we came to understand that afterward Grandma Ida was "never the same," as my mother put it. Grandma herself never talked about the tragedy. Neither did Grandpa, but he joked with us anyway.

So I felt I knew Grandpa Jack better than I did Grandma Ida. She seemed more distracted, more in another time and place, a time and place when refrigerators were—her word, always—"iceboxes" and you never went outside in your "housecoat." (Hers was light pink seersucker.) She wore a small, demure, boxy black hat and white gloves when she went out, which was to say to Manhattan's Metropolitan Museum of Art.

But Grandma Ida, I loved your ladylike ways! Thank you for all the refinements you brought into my life, beginning that forever-remembered school vacation week when I got to stay alone with you and Grandpa Jack. It's because of you that I tasted a certain kind of delicious nameless pudding and still love V-8 juice, black olives and avocados, a vegetable with a peel as mottled as the covers of the black-and-white grade-school composition books of Daddy's that you'd kept. I'd never seen an avocado before you stood paring one over the sink in your small white kitchen. (My mother wouldn't buy them when I asked; she said they were too expensive, but I suspected she really didn't think they were Jewish enough.)

It wasn't just new and, to me, exotic foods that I came to love in your simple, Camay soap–scented apartment. Thank you, too, for giving me my first art lessons, showing me how to use the points and sides of colored pencils. You taught me shading and perspective and even let me experiment with your beloved oils on the easel near the window in your and Grandpa's bedroom. It was the most peaceful feeling in the world to feel the afternoon slip into twilight, smelling that first great but then headachy oil paint smell as the white bedspreads on the mahogany twin beds turned creamy in the dreamy, fading late-afternoon light. From time to time, I'd look out the window at the train tracks, barely visible through the trees and long grass behind your apartment building, and occasionally I'd hear the whistle of the train, which seemed distant although it seemed so near. Kind of like you.

My mother had told me that you took those oils to Manhattan on the subway and would sit in the Met, painstakingly copying the Old Masters in trip after trip until you'd painted what they'd painted. She explained that the pictures you'd painted that hung in her and my father's bedroom were just like famous pictures in the museum.

When I asked you how you did this, you showed me your trick: graph paper. See, you said, you divide the whole picture into grids (you had to explain what a grid was), then reproduce the bigger picture grid by grid, tiny square by tiny square. Because, *ketzeleh*, you said, a whole picture is too big to take on all at once, you'd feel like you could never finish it, and you wouldn't know where to start. It's a lot easier if you take it piece by piece, like this—you showed me the teeny part of the painting you were working on—and start at an edge. . . . See, it's easy to finish a little square and then another and another, and that way, eventually, you finish painting the whole picture.

Before you know it?, I asked you.

No, you said, not before you know it. It takes *patience*.

While I can't honestly thank you for teaching me patience—I have it when it comes to some things, like writing, but not a whole lot of others—the idea of tackling a daunting project or problem, task by task, grid by grid, is something I'm forever grateful to you for. You're right, Grandma; nothing seems too huge or overwhelming when you divide it into smaller, sequential parts. And when you do that, not only do you find the energy and courage to begin, but you find the inspiration to finish. Thank you for showing me how big goals are attainable when you make them the culmination of a logical process.

And thanks for taking me to the Metropolitan Museum for the very first time too. With that special trip, during that special week, you and Grandpa Jack opened up the world of art and history to me in a way I hadn't felt while learning about them in school. When you showed me my first Mary Cassatt and told me a woman had painted it, I was as excited and proud as if she'd been a friend of yours.

The Renoirs! I've seen *The Luncheon of the Boating Party* many, many times since that thrilling day, and I think of you and Grandpa Jack every time with a thank you that makes my heart soar, remembering. Wherever I happen to be when I see it, I'm back at the Met, even when I *am* at the Met, standing between my tall grandpa and my smallish grandma, looking up and understanding the story of a merry moment in another time, another place, told forever with paints like Grandma's.

I wish we could go together to the National Gallery of Art, in Washington.

It wasn't just art you both helped me discover.

Whenever we came to visit, Grandpa Jack would let us wind your precious wooden music box, with the fragrant inside compartment (always empty), which played "The Isle of Capri" over and over. He'd also let us touch and turn over—very carefully—the three fossils he kept on one of the middle shelves in the high, glass-fronted, dark wood secretary in your living room. (I'd never heard of a piece of furniture called a secretary before.) Grandpa also had shells. To this day I have an affinity for a certain kind of white, brown and black speckled shell, the curve of which fits snugly into a child's palm, begging to be safely enclosed by her fingers. Grandpa Jack, an accountant and lifelong New York City dweller, mysteriously knew about ferns too.

So I'm grateful to you, Grandpa, for your lessons about natural forms and for letting me hold both their wonder and their comfort in my hand. You were as interesting when you were serious as you were when you were funny.

I was in junior high when you and Grandma Ida moved to an apartment in Stamford, where you were near enough to come for supper and Ed Sullivan on Sunday nights. Thank you for staying late one of those nights to help me memorize "The Rime of the Ancient Mariner" for my ninth-grade English class with that bad witch of a teacher: *Instead of the cross, the Albatross/ About my neck was hung.* That's pretty much the way I felt about *her,* but you pointed out that if she was teaching us Coleridge (and Keats), how bad could she be? Education, you said, just like Daddy did, is the most important thing to equip yourself with in this unfair world, a world where life didn't "coddle" you. As you put it, it smacked you around.

But you made me laugh even when you were gloomy. One Sunday night, you taught me this song:

"Oh, how we danced on the night we were wed, I needed a wife like a hole in the head."

I'm beginning to realize here that I must have been your best audience, but you were mine too. As moody and sarcastic as you could be with my father and Aunt Stefanie (Grandma was right; I did have "big ears"), with me you were just humorous. I've since found that it's always easy——too easy—to be at your best with people who worship you. I'm glad my parents let me worship you while you were alive, because, it's true, no one else in my family quite understood, the way you did, how my mind worked.

"What's this curly thing?" my parents wanted to know, scanning a picture I'd painted of my room. "That's an aerial view of her piggy bank," you told them. "Isn't it, my sub-deb?" "Sub-deb" was your term for letting me know you could see my body changing, preparing to grow into a young lady's—hence the term debutante.

Thank you for "getting" me, Grandpa Jack!

Things—even my memories—were never the same after you died in 1973, my junior year of high school, from a massive heart attack. You were only seventy-two, the first of my four grandparents to die. It was only in the ensuing years that I heard about some really terrible things you'd done, to my father, to Aunt Stefanie, to Grandma Ida—to everyone, it seems, but the grandchildren you adored, who adored you back.

I'm grateful that those important family stories were kept shut away for as long as they were.

Soon after you died, Grandma Ida began to go further back to other places and other times more often, and stay longer. Her petite body stayed as demure as ever, right up until she died at age 95, but dementia floated in her mind as smoke once had in her kitchen and finally filled its every crevice. I realized once, looking at her with her eyes closed, that I was looking at myself, with her Wagner nose, as an old woman. I'm grateful to have some part of her still, if only in the way I look.

But I do have something real of both of yours that's so much a part of the Grandma Ida and Grandpa Jack I knew the best and longest, in that other place and time when the Forest Hills apartment was a world of discovery and delight. Thank you for the secretary that stands in my living room today.

And thank you for making me a tea drinker. I always take mine with both of Grandpa's dispositions.

Love,

Your eldest grandchild, Pamela

Dear Ross Bagdasarian,

It's never really Christmas for me until I hear three things on my car radio: John Lennon and Yoko Ono singing "So This Is Christmas," Bruce Springsteen doing "Santa Claus Is Coming to Town," and Alvin and the Chipmunks with that real guy, squealing whatever that Chipmunks Christmas song is called. You know. That one.

I hope you're the right person to thank for Alvin and the Chipmunks. I wasn't sure, but I remembered your name from the credits on the cartoon, and I'm pretty sure you were executive producer, because I saw that credit every week for God knows how long. (Clearly, I needed to get a life way before people started saying that.)

If it *was* you, thanks for thinking up the Chipmunks. I have to hand it to you for such a purely silly idea. Alvin and the Chipmunks epitomizes the true greatness in the kind of creative thinking that comes from just sitting around with your friends. It's so much less obvious than the dogs barking "Jingle Bells" too.

I always wondered how the idea came to you. Inhaling helium balloons? Playing 45s at 78 just for the heck of it and then thinking, Hey, I bet I could make a fortune packaging this as a trio of singing chipmunks? Whose voices were the Chipmunks? Was that as big a secret as the identity of the person who masquerades as Barney? What were the recording and mixing sessions like? Did everyone involved laugh all the time?

What especially left its mark on me was the idea that being grown-up and going to work could be so much fun. My dad worked for IBM; he wore dark suits, white shirts and ties every single day. When he got home, he always looked as if his shoes hurt. It amazed me to think that someone else's father worked for *Alvin*. You probably came home in a better mood.

So even though I'm writing to thank you for, among other things, that immortal line from the Chipmunks' Christmas song, *"I still want a hula hoop,"* I'm also writing to thank you for putting in my head the notion that you could be a grown-up and get paid for thinking up things that made you laugh your head off every day. I bet a whole new generation of kids have also figured this out from watching *The Simpsons*. You're the baby boomers' Matt Groening.

I realize you're probably not supposed to choose a career based on whether it cracks you up, but in the end that's what I did.

Thanks for all the squeals and giggles.

Sincerely,

Pam Janis

Dear Marlo Thomas,

Thank you for being one of my best-loved cultural role models as *That Girl*, Ann Marie.

As my role model, you followed Sally Field and preceded Mary Tyler Moore. I mean Sally Field as Gidget, not the Flying Nun; I was Jewish and suspected that God wouldn't be wild about my liking Sister Bertrille too much.

Though I'm still looking for my Don Hollinger, the fact that Ted Bessell played Mary Richards's boyfriend, too, truly blurred the lines between art and art for me. I figured that Don Hollinger must have seen some horrible crime being committed after his divorce from Ann Marie in New York and was moved to Minneapolis in the witness protection program as "Joe," where he met Mary. It was the only way the casting made sense.

I loved *That Girl*.

Little girls who watched TV in the '60s didn't tune in for lifestyle ideas for when they'd be grown-ups; if we did, we wouldn't have been watching *My Three Sons*, too. But *That Girl* made us think. It was the first show with a woman in it who we recognized in ourselves. I wonder how many girls watching you thought, like me, Wow, she's got a fun life; I want to be like her. Who could think that about Lucy, Aunt Bea or Mrs. Howell?

What a breakthrough show *That Girl* was for all those girls! For me especially, judging from my fifth-grade class picture, with my shoulder-length dark brown flip, bangs and Ann Marie smile. Plus, Ann Marie had the same problem I did: two first names. Whenever someone said, "Janis is your *last* name?" I wondered, Does Ann Marie get this all the time, too?

There's a great *That Girl* episode in which you have a dream that you have to get on Noah's Ark with a mate. Your father, Lew Marie, is at your door as Noah, wearing a biblical robe and holding a staff. "You have to decide," he warns as the flood comes closer. I don't think my mother has any idea that I took the show's story line to heart the way I did. She thinks I just came up with the line "He's nice, but I wouldn't get on an ark with him" to describe my more *nebbish* dates.

Thanks for setting my standards for companionship, though. And for delivering the message to do what you love, on your own, with exuberance, despite parental worries and an uncertain future.

When I was just out of college, working at NBC, I'd walk up Sixth Avenue to ABC, to the corner in the opening shots of the show, and mentally thank you.

So, finally, now that I'm in my forties and Ann Marie is, I'd guess, in her early sixties, I'd like to officially thank you for having played her so perfectly. You made her more than a TV sitcom character; she was as real as diamonds, daisies, snowflakes.

Sorry to learn of your and Don's divorce.

Sincerely,

Pam Janis

Dear Dr. Danoff,

I've kept in touch with you since you were our family's pediatrician largely through a group of dedicated communicators who moved from Stamford years ago but still get the Temple Sinai Bulletin. My mother is one of them.

I heard that you left private practice some years ago and became a father of neonatal medicine, as it were, in southern Connecticut. Also that your second, concurrent career as an artist has been blooming along since you started painting while I was still in high school.

By that time you'd expanded your practice to include Adolescent Medicine, to accommodate all the kids who'd grown into teenagers with you as their doctor and who didn't want anyone else touching them when they were sick. I miss those visits to your office on Summer Street when you'd stick a pointy light in my ear and tell me which vegetables were growing in the garden there.

The word "cauliflower" still cracks me up.

I'm actually writing to you concerning my ears. These days, anyone who strolls into a mall with $5 can get their ears pierced, but—oh, brother—what a big, complicated, teary deal it was for me and my sister Caroline to get ours pierced the year I was in sixth grade and she was in fourth. We had the world's most unreasonable parents: parents who couldn't see that everyone but *us* had pierced ears. They told us no, because they thought it was "barbaric." (To me, my brother Gordon's bris was what was barbaric. *"Mazel tov?"* Were those people kidding?)

Caroline and I bickered about everything else under the

sun, from who got to sit in the front seat to who got to jump in the leaf pile first—I was the oldest, was there really a question here?—but on ear-piercing we stood united. So, with both of us braying for social acceptance, my parents considered and reconsidered the options. Finally my father said, "See what Stu Danoff thinks."

I don't know what you said to them, but this letter is to thank you for piercing our ears.

We wore the gold studs with the fourteen-karat posts that we had to twist in our ears for exactly two weeks— I'm wearing them in my sixth-grade school picture, prominently set off by the Twiggy haircut—after which my parents forbade hoops and dangly earrings until well into junior high.

You couldn't have known this, but in addition to my lifelong love of earrings, you gave me a great gift in that shared experience with my sister.

For all the "Play nicelys" we heard in our childhood, we never really did get along until much later. Now that she's a mom, excelling at the one thing the oldest can't do just because she's the oldest, I've come to admire her despite our still very different personalities.

Through all the ages and stages of our long relationship, one thing we have always had in common is our Ears by Danoff. As different as Caroline and I are, you can tell by the pinpoint holes in precisely the same place on our earlobes that she and I are sisters. The last time I saw her, in Paris, where she lives now, her life as far away from mine in every way possible, we were both wearing dangly silver earrings that could have been sisters themselves.

I just wanted to thank you for always reminding us that we are too.

Love,

Pam Janis

P.S.: Now that she's married and has a three-year-old, I expect the same discussion will start up in Caroline's household any year now, and it will be even more heated: she has a boy.

Dear Dr. Martin Luther King Jr.,

Every time I see the footage of your "I Have a Dream" speech, with the cutaways to the mesmerized crowd of listeners hoping for a better, more decent, more equal life in our country, I get chills. Your goodness and courage and power come through even grainy black-and-white film more than three decades old.

I've often wondered how history would have been altered had you lived; I am sure it would be different. I couldn't say how, but watching and remembering what I can remember of you—I was twelve when you were killed—I know two things: the United States lost a true hero, and there has been no one like you since.

But I want you to know something: the last year you were alive, you changed my sixth-grade class. Up until then, kids like me in North Stamford didn't know Negroes (our parents' term; "black" didn't come until junior high) except for Otto, our school bus driver, and the ladies who came from downtown on the High Ridge bus to clean our houses some days.

That changed in sixth grade. Kids like us who looked like you came on school buses, and I made a great friend that year. Her name was Wanda Welcome, and we sat next to each other. Once, when our teacher told us about tapeworms in science, we both got so scared and grossed out that we started screaming and hugged and hugged like that would keep tapeworms from ever getting inside either one of us. Then we were both so surprised that we'd done that, our shrieks turned into giggles. Our teacher stopped us with her "I'M WAITING FOR *YOU* TO PAY ATTENTION" look, but Wanda and I snuck smiles to each other all afternoon until our different buses came to take us home. Hers came earlier than mine; she had a longer ride.

Wanda was fun and nice, and her name made you think of a magician full of surprises; what more could you want in a friend? I had no idea things could be more complicated than that.

The school day after the night you were killed, our teacher told us about you (she was the teacher my father called a "peacenik") and everyone stared at Wanda as though she'd known you personally, feeling the weight of the day as *her* loss. I guessed if she hadn't come to school that day, like when that boy's father died in an accident, we would have written nice notes to her at home.

No one realized it was everyone's loss.

Thank you, Dr. King, for bringing my friend Wanda into my class and for not waiting, but calling on all of us to first pay attention to that tapeworm racism and then starve it.

With gratitude,

*P*am Janis

Dear Helene Liebowitz,

Hi! I know: the last note you ever got from me read DOLAN SUCKS and was written in teeny, looped script on notebook paper, folded into at least eight tiny squares and pushed across the fake oak home economics kitchen table when the teacher wasn't looking.

I can't remember whether we actually took home ec together or whether it was just in homeroom that we sat side by side at table 5, the last table in the row set in front of the five kitchens. We sat at the last table, farthest from the double door, not by choice but because we happened to be the first students to drift in that first day and Miss M. was seating the class at the tables from right to left.

So in a way you were stuck with me, but that didn't mean you had to be my friend, or even be nice to me. Hardly anybody else in that awful junior high school was. My really good friends were at Turn-of-River. But since my street was a school district border, I had to leave them for the daily Dolan torture of horrid kids who hounded me for being a dog.

And those were the generous ones; at least they yelled corrective suggestions for my perpetually bad Dutch Boy haircut. All during junior high, my father saved money— he said for my college education—by styling my head himself, using a Home Barber kit. Thanks to his thrift in this regard, I went to not only Smith but also therapy. Ultimately, I found the Lord, as in Lord & Taylor's Chevy Chase beauty salon, and have forgiven all my Dolan enemies who censured my hair, except that horrible girl who herself looked like Ringo Starr and also added to my misery every Passover when she called the cafeteria's jeering attention to my Baggied matzohs.

I've even forgiven the kids who regularly offered to break my pink cat's-eyes glasses and now only wish that they'd done it. Maybe then my parents would have let me get different frames. Unfortunately, the kids wanted to break my face too. (Thank God—and thank you to my uncle Howard Bernstein, the ophthamologist—for the contact lenses in ninth grade.)

At least those kids *noticed* me. Many others pretended I didn't exist. Even my two friends from elementary school who *did* go to Dolan all but dropped me when it became apparent I was lagging hopelessly behind them in the Tampax/Maidenform department. They started sitting together on the bus, and before you knew it, I was gone from their social radar. I mean, they had boyfriends! Once they even wrote a song about them. I can't remember to pack a shower cap when I travel, but I remember that song. Don't make me sing it. And, boy, do I remember being shunned in eighth grade.

I've never forgotten what a good friend you were to me that year.

How did we become friends? I remember that you were very funny and always had me laughing in homeroom in the morning, no matter who was about to wound me that day, and in the afternoon, no matter who had. Like me, you were on the skinny side, and though you had a shape and I didn't—a fact of which I was reminded at least 431 times in the hallway during every class change—you never made a big deal about it. (Here are the questions of the decade for me: How did Kate Moss make it through junior high? Could I have been a supermodel if the '70s were the '90s? Would I be popular as an eighth grader today?)

In those days one gender took shop; the other, home ec. But Dolan's boys and girls united on one subject: my "bad body." I wrote a story in high school about how Dolan's sewing class depressed me because when we made jumpers, all the other girls had darts to iron. You were the only girl with darts who was nice enough to assure me that Simplicity junior-size patterns were just a matter of time. While my mother's phrase "late bloomer" invariably wilted me, you were as friendly to me as if I were blooming on track with everyone else.

We laughed about various teachers. We talked endlessly—first in homeroom and then past midnight with Noxzema-scrubbed faces at our sleepovers—about the popular kids, trying to analyze what Nancy Murray and Nancy Berg had that put them in the in crowd and what we lacked that relegated us to the fringes. (I thought maybe it was our one-in-the-class names and decided if I ever had a daughter, I'd give her a "popular" name: Nancy, Karen, Patty.)

Did I ever tell you that I once tried to eavesdrop on a conversation some popular girls were having? We were outside; it must have been a gym class. They were sitting in a group on the grass near the fence. I thought if I could hear what they talked about when they were together, we'd know what to say to be popular. I strolled by (naturally, I was by myself), trying not to look interested in them, just as that tall-but-not-tall-enough-to-be-laughed-at girl with the straight, silky, long brown hair, the hair I wanted so much, reached behind herself, scratched and said, "My ass itches."

So *that's* what the popular girls talked about.

I wonder what happened to the Nancys. My mother said the fast crowd would burn out early; she always lied to make me feel better. On the other hand, if they did become brain surgeons or rocket scientists on top of having been popular in junior high school, I don't think I'd want to know.

It's funny, when I look back at eighth grade, I feel almost nostalgic for the time in our lives when the worst thing in the world was to not be popular. I'm sure we've both raised the bar a bit since, but it's hard to imagine ever feeling as deeply and chronically miserable as 1970 B.C. (Before Contacts). But, of course, this was twenty years or more before California led the nation in making "self-esteem" part of the public school experience. Or before computer-assisted design programs let you glimpse what you'd look like ten or more years beyond Clearasil. Or before kids like me could sue kids who made fun of them for "sexual harassment" and "abuse." And the school system would be held responsible for allowing it!

When I think of the fortune I could have made . . .

Even though twenty-seven years have passed since I passed you my last note, there's really nothing new in this one. Only the tense has changed: DOLAN SUCKED.

We moved into different social circles in high school, but your sense of humor and kindness in eighth grade made a lifelong impression on me. I've never forgotten it and wanted you to know.

Thank you, Helene, for being my friend when no one else would.

Love,

Pam Janis, alias "P.J."

P.S.: If Miss M. sees us, EAT THIS NOTE!

Dear Cousin Brucie and Dan Ingram,

When 77-WABC in New York was Musicradio, not
Talkradio, your voices brought me the Beatles, the
Supremes, the Beach Boys, Stevie Wonder, the Stones . . .
all of it.

Hearing WABC for the first time—I was seven—was
like traveling to a new country, a place where parents
didn't go and didn't have to take you. You could get there
by yourself, just by turning a dial, and there would be
Dan Ingram after school, Cousin Brucie after dinner.

Long after I was supposed to be asleep, I'd lie with the
covers pulled over my head, listening to Cousin Brucie's
show through the tangled earphone of my black hand-
sized transistor radio.

I defected to FM eventually but was inexplicably sad
when I read in the early '80s that WABC was changing to
an all-talk format.

You were the two guys who brought rock music into
my life on a daily basis. Would the music have been as
great at first without your words, voices and energy? I
don't know, but since they're all forever tangled in my
mind's earpiece anyway, I wanted to thank you for those
special Musicradio 77-WABC days and nights.

Sincerely,

Pam Janis

Dear John, Paul, George, and Ringo,

Thank you for all the great music that scored this sequence of events in my life:

First, my family watched you on Ed Sullivan, and while I was screaming during "She Loves You," my father told me to quit it, saying that no one would remember who the Beatles were in three months. Three months later, he said I'd "outgrow" you. Then he declared he wouldn't spend money on "noise," so would I please stop pestering him to buy your records, and I gave up on him *and* my mother, who always sided with my father. The world's most misunderstood child, I stomped off through the woods in back of our house to listen to *The Beatles' Second Album* at Kathy Stumpe's, whose parents were more progressive than mine.

Next, I saved all my allowance money (my father had been sure I'd spend it first) to buy my first Beatles LP. It took a while—by the time I'd saved eight dollars, the current Beatles album was *HELP!* Boy, was my father mad.

Then he said, "Don't be ridiculous," when I brought up the Shea Stadium concert. He accused me of being eleven; I informed him I was almost twelve. He was immovable. (My one regret in life is not getting to go to that concert. I couldn't care less that I missed Woodstock, never went to Florida on spring break, and had no real estate to sell in the '80s, but *damn,* I wanted to go to that concert.)

My dad's anti-Beatle years are kind of a blur for a while after that, coinciding as they did with his pro-Vietnam years, but I do remember his reaction when he read what John said about you being more popular than Jesus Christ. With no apparent irony whatsoever, my father bellowed, *"Jesus Christ!"*

Then, oh man, you should have seen the look on his

face when I was in eighth grade and had to tell him I'd entered a 77-WABC radio essay contest, twenty-five words or less, on why the Beatles shouldn't break up.

I had to tell him, because I had won. And I couldn't get to New York with my then–best friend, Helene Liebowitz (Kathy Stumpe had moved to Milwaukee), for my prize, two seats at the screening of the movie *Let It Be,* without his driving us.

He was in his reclining chair in his study. I knocked on the door, as he'd trained us to do, even though it was open.

I broke the news.

He lowered his *New York Times* and said, "You did *what?*" I explained.

He said, "And what, exactly, did you win?" When I told him "Tickets to a Beatles movie," he asked sarcastically if that was *last* prize. I reported it was first. The movie was a week from Saturday, I added helpfully.

He put his newspaper down and said, "Show me what you wrote."

"Well, okay," I told him, "but it's more than twenty-five words."

"How many words is it?"

"Three hundred twenty-five."

"How did you win if you went over by three hundred words?"

"Well, I wrote a note to the judges at the end, saying that if the essay was too long and they had to disqualify me, I'd sum it all up in twenty-five words—actually, it was twenty-four—and they should just count that."

I could tell he was trying not to laugh.

"Let me see your summary."

I handed him the crossed-out first draft of my contest entry in blue BiC ink on yellow legal paper. He turned it over and read aloud: *"The Beatles shouldn't break up because there is no one like them. They represent my generation like no one else has, can and will."*

"Has, can and will," he repeated. "Sounds like a law firm."

I waited. What would he do? He hated the Beatles but was always encouraging my writing. I had him by the ballpoint. But he *really* hated the Beatles. I couldn't call it. Oh, how I hoped . . .

Finally, my father said, "When an editor—or whoever—gives you a word limit, you have to stick to it. You can't go even a word over."

"Okay," I said.

He gave me one of his surprising Daddy grins.

"Sheesh," he said. "Insanity is inherited. You get it from your kids. When are you supposed to be there?"

When I was in high school, the American writer Joyce Maynard wrote a book called *Looking Back: A Chronicle of Growing Up Old in the Sixties*, in which she likened hearing the Beatles to discovering a new color.

I've never forgotten that description (thanks, Joyce Maynard), because I've never been able to improve on it.

Thanks, Fab Four, for your miraculous sound that colored my growing up so completely that even today it recalls for me my father's fury.

And for representing my generation like no one else has, can and will.

Your fan,

Pamela Janis

P.S.: I Love You.

"Anticipation . . .
is making me late,
is keeping me waiting. . . ."
—CARLY SIMON

Dear Mom,

I had every intention of writing you this letter on my birthday to thank you for having me, among other things, but I got sidetracked, and so this is a day late. As it happens, I was also a dollar short at Safeway today. I know things like this worry you, but really, "freelance" is *not* a code word for "unemployed."

As far as being late goes, I guess this is in keeping with the spirit of my birth, when I showed up nine days later than you'd planned. So the first thing I want to thank you for is not starting my life without me.

Judging from my baby pictures, I was laughing from the moment Dr. Schnall slapped me in the delivery room at Mount Sinai. What were you *telling* me in utero—talk about a captive audience—or during the next nine months before I first spoke? I've long suspected that the best female Jewish comedic talent was playing the Pablum Belt in the '50s. I look at my first-year photographs and wonder, Was Mom doing her ape-face rendition of "Abba Dabba Dabba" *that* far back?

Your explanation for being so entertaining is "I grew up in the Depression." We always wondered why that didn't make you depressed.

You couldn't have enjoyed the screwball comedies of your youth more than I enjoyed mine. Maybe because the only other "Lucille" we'd ever heard of was Lucille Ball, or maybe because things seemed to happen to you that didn't happen to anyone else—let me just remind you that the only time *Jeopardy* was preempted on TV in New York, New Jersey and Connecticut in the history of the world, it seemed, was the day in 1969 you were on it—whatever it was, your children thought you were a scream.

The way you mixed English and Yiddish sent us into fits of giggles. You told us stories like the time Grandma Helen was talking on the phone so long that after getting a busy signal for hours, Grandpa Max sent her a telegram from his belt factory a subway ride away that read, *Yente, get off the phone.* You recited *The Owl and the Pussycat* from memory, doing all the voices. You knew all the skips on the Peter and the Wolf record and said, "Grandfather came out, came out, came out, came out . . . ," until one of us got up and tapped the needle. If you'd had a singing voice (though the fact that you didn't never stopped you from singing) and not lived at the stove, you would have been the female version of the consummate entertainer you loved, Danny Kaye.

Like Danny Kaye in *Hans Christian Andersen,* you told stories to everyone—timid children, scary teachers, important men Daddy knew, the occasional celebrity—and they always listened, apparently as captivated as I first was, sitting in a high chair, eyeing you from the tip of a rubber spoon. "My mother isn't shy," I told my friends after you introduced yourself to Jack Klugman, of *The Odd Couple,* one morning at the front desk of the Jerusalem Hilton, but that doesn't really explain how you got him to send Gordon, Oscar Madison's biggest and at that teenaged time quite possibly messiest fan, a postcard on which he'd scrawled, *Gordon: Get neat!—Jack Klugman.*

That's one of our classic Mom stories, by the way. A classic Mom story is one that makes people say, *"WHAT?!"* As long as I've known you—and this is now forty-one years already—you've been saying things that make people say, *"WHAT?!"* "True story," you say, adding details like "He was wearing a T-shirt and light-colored pants. He didn't look well."

Your gabbing talents are legendary among those who know you—Daddy used to refer to this group as "the immediate world"—but what I remember most clearly about growing up with you as my mother was your gift for ad hoc silliness. I never laughed so hard with you as when I didn't expect to.

You could find—or create—mirth in a moment. One night when I was thirteen, just before Thanksgiving, the house was fast asleep. I heard the hum of the sewing machine and came downstairs to find you at work, bleary-eyed, making a Pilgrim costume for Gordon to wear in his kindergarten play the next day. As I watched, you floored the foot pedal in a roar to finish the cheap, shiny black material's edges, looked up at me with "This had better be the last time I hem a *schmata* for school" merrily emblazoned on your face, triumphantly zoomed down the last stitch, jerked up the machine's silver foot, ripped the trailing thread, yanked the material out and said with finality in Yiddish, *"Ain, svay, dray—ner hubben* a Pilgrim." ("One, two, three, we have a Pilgrim.")

"Ain, svay, dray—ner hubben a Pilgrim." This is still my code phrase for disposing of anything with dispatch. It's what I think as I file a story with minutes to go on deadline, check off a list of errands or phone calls or shove the vacuum cleaner back into the closet: *"Ain, svay, dray—ner hubben* a Pilgrim." Thanks for tucking such a useful and meaningful phrase into my mind, as you would say, "for permanent," Mom. I can honestly say that I don't

know a single other person who ever thinks that. Except, I suspect around every Thanksgiving, you.

Let me just return to my vacuum cleaner here for a moment, because thanks to you, it has been crucial to the development of my worldview. You didn't want me to buy a vacuum cleaner when I was on my own; you told me buying a vacuum cleaner would be bad luck in the marriage department. "A vaccum cleaner should be a wedding present," you said. Finally, in Washington—I'd been on my own for a couple of years already, borrowing peoples' vacuum cleaners like a nut because my mother was superstitious that no one would marry a single woman who owned one, a woman who so obviously didn't need a man to whack cobwebs with a broom, *she could use her mini-blind attachment,* who would want such a woman "for permanent?"—in spite of all the clear evidence you saw in the *New York Times* wedding announcements of my Smith classmates each Sunday that you were right, I went to Sears anyway and bought a Kenmore vacuum cleaner.

I entered the store feeling ludicrously like I was tempting fate and disobeying my mother in the bargain. (I was, but just the second part.) I left the store feeling exactly as I'd felt leaving the gynecologist's office after getting fitted for my first diaphragm. The only difference was that I told you about the vacuum cleaner. "I'm rebelling," I told you. "I'm having premarital dust."

You will read this and say, "I was right. You're such a *chuchem;* tell me: are you married?" No, but now I have an Oreck.

Okay, so clearly I am not writing this letter to thank you for your useful romantic advice or compassion for what you believe is the inevitable consequence of my disregard for it.

In fact, I've had enough of that whole subject from you to last a half-life. This particular dialogue of ours long, long ago outdistanced the myth of Sisyphus in terms of both endurance and futility.

I will say I wish I'd had good news for you in the wedding department somewhere along the way, because it would be wonderful to hear joy and not worry in your voice when we talk.

But see, for myself what's important is gratitude for what I *have*. I mean, last Rosh Hashana, when I had the mammogram scare, I thought I might be *dying*, for goodness' sakes! You can have a great life if you're unmarried, but not if you're dead.

So. When I think about what I want to thank you for, it all has to do with what to me are the *vital* things in life: humor, resiliency, the moxie to cope with loss and death, embracing a cultural heritage, courage, making a home where new and old friends are always welcome and celebrating Thanksgiving, your favorite holiday, every year by going around the table and having everyone present tell what the year has brought for which they're thankful.

What a great tradition! The fact that you started it when we were already in our twenties and life at that point wasn't easy for you as a widow in a nothing job made it especially meaningful. (Oh, my God, remember that job? The associate who tried to recruit you to sell Amway by asking, "Lucille, do you have a dream?" The tedium of it made you cry; the absurdity of it made you laugh.)

Which brings me back to the first thing about you I

remember being glad for, that you showed your children how to see through slightly askew eyes, to laser in on the world's absurdities, thereby making it a vastly fascinating and amusing place stuffed with more surprises even than your Thanksgiving turkeys and pies. I've never been able to explain to people why bed stores and mattress departments, in particular, make my mother laugh uncontrollably, but your kids definitely see the world through Goldfeder eyes, because a roomful of grown people bouncing on beds and then closing their eyes and pretending to be asleep on them cracks *us* up too.

I feel sorry for people who don't know from fun. I feel lucky that my mother is a person who's always known that to have fun, you have to make fun happen. Also that you have a better time in life if you can laugh at yourself once in a while, if not most of the time.

Had you only given me this knowledge—a gift that always compels me to join conga lines—*Dayenu* ("that would have been enough").

Had you only given me enough of a kook's streak to make my life unbelievably interesting and colorful but not enough of one to land me in a hospital, cult or jail, *Dayenu*.

Had you only applied your steel will and elastic spirit to coping with Daddy's sudden death, going to work, selling the Stamford house you loved, and putting all four of us through college, *Dayenu*.

Okay, I won't go through the entire Haggadah; that last one was the most important anyway.

How is it that despite widowhood, job and money stresses, not to mention enough boyfriends of mine to populate Chelm, that mythical town of fools, you've never lost your hope? How is it that your heart, still and always, leaps up when you behold a rainbow in the sky, no matter what *tsouris* the flood before it wreaked?

You've been a lifelong example to me of how courage renews hope—and vice versa—and how everyone always has more of both than they think. I can't thank you enough for that. Also for showing me how telling stories can bring people into your life and home and that you should have plenty for them to eat when they get there.

Thanks for being a mother who came through the Depression knowing that hope and laughter, at least, are free, and for never losing your hope or your laugh. How proud I feel to have a mom whose favorite thing to do, especially come every November, is give thanks.

When I told you about these thank-you notes, I asked you who in *your* life you'd write one to.

"Hmm," you said, thinking about it. "I know—the woman in the candy store who talked Grandma Helen out of the abortion."

"*WHAT?!*"

"True story," you said. "Grandma got pregnant with me by accident. Grandpa wasn't working—they lived over a candy store—and Grandma knew they couldn't afford a third child, so she didn't tell him she was pregnant; instead, she made an appointment to have an abortion. Comes the day, she went downstairs to ask the woman who owned the candy store to watch Uncle Herbie and Aunt Harriet while she went for the abortion. The woman said to her, Helen, don't do it. If anything happens to you, do you think Max will take such good care of the other children as you do? *Think about it, what if something happens to you?* You can *find* money; you think children can find *mothers* so easily?

"Grandma thought about it, *ain, svay, dray,* then decided to have me and went back upstairs. So I would say the woman in the candy store deserves at least a note of thanks from me, wouldn't you?"

So this letter is a thank-you to her too.

You can never wait for the calendar to begin planning for Thanksgiving. When it's still six weeks away, you'll start with the phone calls, inviting, as you say, "all and sundry."

"Do come," you invite Thanksgiving newcomers every year. "The family will be here; I hope you'll join us for assorted fruits and nuts."

Thanks, Mom, for giving me so much to give thanks for every day of the year.

       Love,

       Pamela

Dear Dolly, Susie, Robin, and Linney,

I know so many people who cringe at the thought of their high school reunion that it's almost embarrassing to admit how much I loved Rippowam, but because it was mostly the four of you who made me love school so much, I guess it's okay to say so.

You are the Great Women I've known the longest: Dolly and Robin from Miss Chipouras's tenth-grade English class, and Susie and Linney since Mrs. Brindell's second grade (but since we went to different junior high schools, it was really in Miss Chipouras's class that I rediscovered you both).

As different as our five lives are, whenever we talk, it seems as if no time has passed. We all get busy and months do pass, then there's a message, a note, a photo, a card—and the one who's left it or sent it comes into my focus viscerally first, with a rush of clarity and gratitude on my part even before I begin to hear or read whatever news you're sharing.

My mother says that what stood out to her about us was that we didn't compete; we emulated one another. And it's true, at least for me, not just in school, where you were four of the brightest Class of '74 stars, but in your awareness of what was going on in the world, your self-possession, and your self-respect.

I could thank you for your loyalty to me and to one another over the years, but that doesn't quite capture what it is about you—about us—that makes this group and the individual friendships it's enclosed for more than twenty-five years so unique and joyous.

Dolly: I gazed at your gorgeous cascade of red hair from

the desk behind yours for only a few weeks before you finally turned around to ask me something or borrow a pen or who knows what, but once you did, I recognized a soulmate. A few weeks into the year, Miss Chip began assigning us creative writing essays once a week, and I realized, hearing yours read in class, how awesomely talented you were in addition to being gorgeous, brilliant and funny. Thank you for all the shared dinners and sleepovers and talk and Friendly's french fries and Christmas Eve with your mom's traditional Austrian goose that followed. Thank you for all the free psychotherapy you gave me years before you became a psychologist. Thank you for reintroducing me to your best Turn-of-River chum, Susie.

Susie: You were the smartest kid in Mrs. Brindell's class, so I for one wasn't surprised when you were voted our high school Class Genius (Female). Your intellect blew me away. I was such a one-note student (English); you probed and mastered every subject you studied, from calculus to poetry. You tried so hard to teach me bridge, but I was just so bad in math and could never remember the cards that had already been played. The only thing I remember from all your effort is "Never Trump your partner's ace," and the only reason I remember that is that I had, and you were my partner. Remember how we loved Frankie Valli and the Four Seasons and eventually ended up in a sky box at one of their Madison Square Garden concerts because no one else in your dad's law firm wanted the tickets? (Thanks, Mr. Levitan.) Or the spring school day we played tennis for six periods to make up all the gym classes we'd skipped going to the IHOP to eat sausages "cuddled" in pancakes, as the menu read? We had time to kill that day; classes were virtually nonexistent, because most other seniors were home, getting ready for the prom that night. Thanks for all the things you taught me even before you became a teacher. Thank you for introducing me to Robin.

Robin: You were the one of us who most loved the outdoors, so I'm glad you ended up in Colorado. I admired your gift for foreign languages; you were a star in both French and Spanish (mastering either one was inconceivable to me). Although we spent a fair amount of time laughing in chemistry labs, in the end you were the reason I passed that class. Thank you for all the help. Thank you for the common sense that went far beyond your high school age and still is light-years ahead of most of us (okay, just me). Thank you for being such a good listener. Thank you for sharing your great laugh, along with your lab notes. I love the fact that you have three girls, just like your mom.

Linney: I seem to be the last holdout in a world that calls you "Linda," but Linney became your name to me forever when Mrs. Brindell had two Lindas in her class and so came up with "Linney" for you. Our shared loves were our dogs, your German shepherd, Honey, and my mutt, Curly; James Taylor; and Sara Lee's entire line of freezer cakes. Thank you for the memorable visits we made to Smith together senior year (I was so disappointed when you decided on Brown); your advice and encouragement in everything from dealing with parents to job hunting; and especially this: for giving me my first lessons in gratitude by the way you, even as a teenager, loved your wonderful dad, George, the mom you lost so early, Ann, and then your dad's beloved Ruth.

All four of you made me feel, for the first time, like celebrating the life I'd been given (what can I say, this was post–junior high) and also that I had something to bring to the party. I had no confidence when I entered Rippowam. You're the friends who helped me find mine. How can I ever thank you enough for that?

It was Susie's idea to have a reunion the year we turned forty. What a magical weekend that was. We descended in Cleveland from Ithaca, Denver and Washington, D.C. (Linney, I'm so sorry you couldn't be there.) Thanks, you other three, for picking me up at the airport. After the inevitable rendezvous point screwup and the subsequent paging, we were laughing hysterically before conversation could spill from a single mouth. It was Miss Chipouras's class all over again, except that now you all have children, and some of us color our hair. (Naturally, Dolly, the one whose dad worked for Clairol, doesn't have to.)

I'm all the more grateful for that reunion now, as I write this, a year and a half later.

Because it isn't Miss Chipouras's class anymore. Cancer, divorce, a parent's ongoing mental illness, and the loss of a stepparent have all shadowed us since. We're women in the world in our fifth decades, and it's not as kind a world as it once was.

I'm so grateful we have one another in it.

Thank you, dearest Dolly, Susie, Robin and Linney, for

the years of friendship that began at Rippowam High School and have come far, far beyond.

Love,

Pam

Dear Xaviera Hollander,

I read *The Happy Hooker* in high school in the early '70s when it came out and everyone was talking about the book and you.

My friends Susie, Dolly, Robin and I took turns reading it aloud to one another in Susie's bedroom. We laughed so hard—you made your life sound so funny. I can't say we considered similar career paths, but we sure loved the German shepherd story.

It was a real bummer later when Sidney Biddle Barrows became the Snobby Hooker and every picture of Heidi Fleiss made her the Sullen Hooker. A couple of years ago, it was the Victimized and Revengeful Hookers who gave us *You'll Never Make Love in This Town Again*. You were smart to be the first to figure out that no matter what people say about the nation's morals going to hell in a handbasket, they will read hooker memoirs at the drop of a garter belt.

Your book was good because you had good stories to tell and told them well, not because you came from a Mayflower family, had a Beverly Hills doctor dad, or dished dirt on movie and rock stars. I loved the days when people like you shocked us, when we were all still shockable, by just telling their tales.

I hope you made a ton of money. From the book, I mean.

Thanks for the laughs.

Sincerely,

Pam Janis

Dear Mary Tyler Moore,

An ex-boyfriend of mine once told me that he'd
planned to win me back by taping an entire Nick at Nite
weeklong *Mary Tyler Moore Show* marathon for me, then
throwing in a few *Dick Van Dyke Show* episodes for good
measure. I didn't tell him this, but it probably would have
worked.

It's true: though most of the world has fast-forwarded
to the '90s and Ally McBeal, I still have an affinity for
Mary Richards and Laura Petrie. Anyone in my life over
thirty-five knows this. My *Detroit News* editor, Alan Fisk,
once sent me a Post-it on a bunch of my tear sheets that
read, "You're gonna make it after all." My sister Michele
asked, "Does the *Mary Tyler Moore Show* theme song start
playing when you wake up in the morning?" My friend
Amy Bernstein looked me over after a haircut and said,
"Oh, Rob."

It's too awful to think that I should thank you for
giving me an identity, so I'm writing to thank you instead
for giving the world characters so enduring and endearing
that they created a language and code all their own. If I
were to say on a date, for instance, *"A little song, a little
dance . . . ,"* and the reply is, "Huh?" instead of the
obvious *". . . a little seltzer down your pants,"* then from
somewhere within the deepest recesses of my heart comes
the message: "Mission Control here . . . Abort launch."

How many women in my age group, I wonder, like me
looked at apartments when they were single and shouted,
"I'll take it!" when they saw the one with the cutout-
window kitchen?

Thank you for defining the single, working, friendly,

optimistic, cheery, good-friend woman with *spunk* for so many women now mostly past their thirties, including me. You set our style.

For your undated and unduplicated comedy, I thank you from the crown of my flip to the hem of my Capris.

Sincerely,

Pam Janis

Dear Bethie/Beth/Beth Susan,

Thank you for the suggestion, but if I were to write a book of thank-you letters, I would probably not call it *Thank You to Beth Levine and All Those Other Shleppers*.

I would, however, definitely put you in it.

I would put you in it because I'd want to thank you for being my friend even though you thought I was a snob at first because I wouldn't lend you my contact lens solution from my bulging purse that day after Mr. Harre's history class in tenth grade. I know you still don't believe that I thought contact lens solution was like mascara that way, but thank you anyway for overlooking your first impression and deciding you'd be my friend anyway.

I'd also thank you for all your imaginative stories in the lit review we worked on together in eleventh grade, when I first realized how unbelievably talented a writer you are and how good a friend.

I'd also thank you for bringing me home to your mom and dad junior year, when the top sleepover subject was the "meaningful relationships" we weren't having. But let's not get into that disastrous double date with those upperclassmen. I felt like part of your family (at one point I seriously considered leaving a toothbrush at your house). And I'd thank your wonderful parents, Julian and Carol, Dr. and Mrs. Levine, as I knew them, for letting me sleep over as much as I did. (I miss your dad too. He was the first doctor who asked, during an office visit, if I was under any stress. I thought this was his way of letting me know he knew my parents, but it turns out he knew finals were coming up because *you* were under stress. A great doctor and a great dad—thanks for sharing him, Bethie.)

I might thank you for agreeing, when we were sixteen, to be my bridesmaid when I got married. Hope there's no statute of limitations on that one.

I'd thank you for all the great letters you wrote me from Trinity—do you realize our colleges were forty-five minutes apart? Why were we writing all those letters?

I'd probably mention how helpful you were when I was having trouble in biology freshman year and you coached me over the phone.

It's been twenty-five years already that you've been cracking me up, listening to my stories, telling me yours, reading my stories, sending me yours, ignoring my advice, giving me yours (and I have to admit it, yours is better), comparing notes on the freelance life and who pays on time, sharing the news from Stamford, and all the rest of the stuff that fits into the bulging purse of an old friendship.

So, yes, thank you for all these things, and, if you want, I'll lend you both my contact lens solution and my mascara anytime.

Love,

Pammy/Pam/Pamela Ruth

Dear Allen Drury,

Thank you for writing the novel that changed my life.

I read *Advise and Consent* in tenth grade, not because I had any particular interest in Washington but because as a kid I'd looked at the title on the book's spine on the family room bookshelves and had wondered for years what it meant.

Although I knew nothing of Washington politics, you told such a real story, with such vivid characters—I felt positively devastated when Senator Anderson killed himself—that you convinced me there was no more exciting perch from which to view history in the making than the U.S. Senate. *Advise and Consent* made me want to be a Senate page more than anything, but, alas, only boys could be pages.

Until just a few short months after I read the book.

Before tenth grade was over, there was big news from Washington: girls, too, could be pages. And I wanted to be one of the first. So I applied, along with two hundred other Connecticut high schoolers who'd no doubt read *Advise and Consent,* to the office of our senator, Lowell Weicker.

I didn't get the job, but the other finalists and I did get what has to be the greatest consolation prize of my life. It was called an "internship," but it was really a weeklong immersion into our political process and the capital's culture. I came here for a week and realized the truth in your fiction: Washington *is* the most exciting place in the world. Not because of its esteemed (or goofball) members of Congress but because this is where Congress itself lives, soul as well as body. It can be a maddening place to reside—the center of both the best of individual intentions and the worst of committee renderings—but whatever your politics, to live here is to forever feel your heart quicken at the sight of the U.S. Capitol.

Two things in life never fail to make me misty. One is a press run, that daily celebration of the First Amendment. (Press runs always recall for me Al Neuharth's great description of newspapers as "democracy on the doorstep.") The other is Fourth of July fireworks on the Mall. As many times as I've seen the technicolored bombs bursting in air above and beyond the Washington Monument, as complex and infuriating and stupid as whatever is going on politically at the moment, I see Fourth of July fireworks on the Mall and am reduced to patriotism. Until the dawn's early light or the next health-care horror story, whichever comes first.

I wouldn't have come here if *Advise and Consent* hadn't captured Washington so perfectly and then captured me. I wouldn't have stayed if my roommate during that week's internship, a high schooler from Storrs, Connecticut, named Betsy Page, hadn't years later given me a career lead that led to a life-changing speechwriting association.

When I follow back far enough the chain of events that led to this letter, there's a book on a shelf in the den that went from being above my head to eye level. Who knows what might have happened if I'd instead reached for the book next to it, James Michener's *Hawaii*; I might be penning *him* a thank-you note from a Maui beach.

But here I am in Washington. Thank you for writing *Advise and Consent* and all the great books that followed it in the series. It's amazing what can happen when you read a good book.

Sincerely,

Pam Janis

P.S.: Only five months after I wrote this letter, I came across your obituary in the *Washington Post*. How I wish I'd thanked you sooner.

Dearest Betsy,

Greetings from our nation's capital—yes, *still*. Thanks to you, I never left Washington!

Our chance pairing as hotel roommates during the week we were high school Washington interns was a turning point whose impact can be measured only from a distance of years. I knew at the time what a fun, optimistic, bright, happy person you were—the ideal roommate!—but who could have guessed how much I'd come to owe you for my career here?

I remember that after we laughed our heads off every single night in Washington for a week (and were tired every single day), we just *had* to continue being friends, even though you lived in Storrs, and I lived in Stamford. So, in the months before we got our driver's licenses, we took the train back and forth for weekends (a whole new concept in sleepovers) and called each other long-distance. My parents adored you, and so did my sisters and brother. You were my first friend who lived in another city; how exciting that was for me.

And how I loved your family! Thanks, Dr. and Mrs. Page (I feel like I'm still too young to call you Ellis and Betty) for embracing me as Betsy's friend even though that always involved driving. I remember us listening to music with your older brother, Tim, and younger brother, Ricky, in Tim's attic bedroom and feeling like they were my brothers too. And I remember the big plans we made for being roommates again in Washington someday, after college, with jobs on the Hill and pink, yellow and green curtains (our agreed-upon favorite colors) on the windows.

But there I was, in my New Jersey newsroom, opening

my mail one day: Uh-oh, what's this? A wedding invitation from *Betsy?* Darn, she went and got herself another roommate.

So, you were in Washington years before me. When I finally moseyed on down here, I found a job (not on the Hill). I can't remember now what yours was.

We were talking one day after the consulting firm I'd been working for "downsized." (I hate that made-up word; it always makes me think of "capsized," which is usually closer in meaning to what's actually happened.) The first thing all the books say to do is call everyone you know, looking for ideas and "contacts" (another Conehead word). So I called you. Help, I said, I need job leads.

You gave me the name of a friend you'd met at a summer "think tank" job (that one is pure Washington; now a think tank *top,* that would be a concept). Give her a call, you said. She knows *everyone.*

So I went off for what's called the "informational interview." ("I need some information: would you hire me?") And darned if your friend hadn't just heard that the new publisher of *USA Today,* a woman, was looking for a speechwriter.

The rest of the story is that I got that job, and it was the most rewarding career step I've ever taken. (I wish I could remember who it actually was that steered me across the Potomac to *USA Today,* but I know *you* will, so please thank her for me.)

If I hadn't read *Advise and Consent* and applied to be a Senate page; if you hadn't applied too; if we hadn't both gotten the internship instead; if we hadn't been assigned the same hotel room; if we hadn't become friends; if we hadn't both come to Washington in our twenties . . . this is how happenstances determine our lives.

Or is it fate? Against all logic or law, we somehow end up meeting the people who determine the direction we take at life's crossroads, and only as we look back do those particular steps forward seem inevitable. The road your generous help led me down feels so right that I have to believe our paths' crossing wasn't happenstance at all.

The impact that you've had on my life and my work, Betsy, continues to this day. I don't know where you are, but I know I wouldn't be where I am—and I don't just mean in Washington—if it weren't for you.

Well, I suppose if you look at it from one point of view, you never know what can come from sharing a bathroom with someone for a week.

Thank you for being so neat in there, Bets.

And thank you for pointing me in the right life's direction.

Love,

Pam

TO MY TEACHERS AT RIPPOWAM HIGH SCHOOL, 1971–1974:

> MISS BEA CHIPOURAS, ENGLISH
>
> MISS MARTHA WEISSBERG, RUSSIAN LIT
>
> MRS. PATSY FAGAN, CREATIVE WRITING
>
> MR. JOSIAH BRIDGE, AP ENGLISH
>
> DR. SARAH ANNE CASSADY, CHEMISTRY
>
> MR. WALTER PLANT, BIOLOGY
>
> MR. DAVID MAZZA, AMERICAN HISTORY
>
> MR. JOHN THEALL, MATH
>
> MRS. SHIRLEY SWAIN, GEOMETRY
>
> MISS PAMELA PERCIVAL, GYM
>
> MR. CHARLES ROBERTSON, JOURNALISM
>
> MR. PETE MESSINA, PUBLIC SPEAKING
>
> MR. BRUCE TUCCI, HOMEROOM
>
> MRS. ROBERTA PRITZKER, GUIDANCE

Dear all of you,

Before the Misses were Ms.es, before the flood of baby boomers ran dry and they closed the school, before I ever published a word, before I was out in the world, before I knew anyone, before I knew anything, I had teachers. Great teachers. Teachers so intellectually gifted, so tuned in to high schoolers, and so insistent that we learn and love their subjects, that we tried as hard as we could to do just that because we *wanted* to, even though some of us fell awfully short in the science, math and gym departments and can pretty much count "passing" as their lifetime achievement in those areas.

I just wanted you to know that you've all been in my

memory and heart since Rippowam. Thank you for your deepest imprints on both.

Love always,

The student with probably the most skewed math and verbal $SATs$ to ever come out of Stamford's public schools.

P.S.: A special thank-you to Mr. Bridge for this prescient scribbled comment in my Class of '74 yearbook:

So you think you can write, do you?!
Remember, most great writers were usually a nuisance in other respects.

Dear Cousin Gerald,

I know that for years you've been trying to spread the word that most people call you "Jerry," that's it's *okay* to call you Jerry, or your Hebrew name, Yehuda, that you'd *prefer* being called either one or the other. Alas, we were born into an extended family where at least two generations have mostly insisted on using the full given names of all its members and in so doing have hinted strongly that nicknames are for *goyim*, along with cotillions, horseback riding, and Volkswagens.

Let's make a deal: I'll call you Jerry or Yehuda, as you prefer, if you'll call me Pam and not Pamela.

Do you remember that when I got into Smith, you sent me roses? I do. How could I forget?! They were the very first flowers anyone ever sent me.

What a great event that was!

I was home from school after a giddy day; my guidance counselor had told me I'd gotten in, and the letter from the college—the thick envelope everyone hopes for—was waiting for me on the kitchen table. (Of course, my mother had opened it already. I've had ferrets who were less curious than Lucille.)

Mom evidently had already spread the word. The doorbell rang and it was . . . roses! My mother and I looked at the flowers in wonder. A dozen red American Beauties, some of them in full bloom, others waiting to unfold later in that most thrilling week. Who could they be from? I plucked the miniature white envelope from the vase's thorny thicket before my mother could open any more of my mail that day.

"They're from Cousin Gerald and Shelly!" I exclaimed.

The card you enclosed still touches me: you, the youngest of my mother's cousins and the first family member to go to law school, congratulating *me* for being the first family member to get into one of those schools that the *goyim* sent their kids to.

If I didn't convey to you then how special and important your roses were to me, I want to do so now. To this day, any cut vegetation delivered to my door recalls the surprise and pleasure of that first dozen. And because I remember how special and important your roses made *me* feel, I love to *send* flowers! Anyone who's ever gotten a bunch or bouquet from me should know they were really from *you*.

Thanks to you and Shelly for increasing my excitement about getting into Smith twelve-fold with your thoughtfulness.

Love,

*P*am

A proud moment in 1973: I had just turned seventeen. It was a warm August day, and downstairs in the kitchen my mother was on the phone with my Aunt Harriet. I knew this because whenever the phone rang in our house, whoever didn't get it yelled, *"Who is it?"* and whoever did yelled back the answer. There was a lot of yelling in our house: *"Aunt Harriet! Aunt Bernice! Uncle Herbie! Grandma Helen! Beth Levine! Aunt Stefanie! Grandpa Jack! Sue Levitan! Some man from the temple for Daddy!"*

As I clopped down the stairs in my blue Dr. Scholl's to retrieve my Dippity-Doo from the powder room, or some such stupid thing (I was always trying to straighten my frizzy hair—once Beth Levine tried ironing it on her mom's ironing board; it didn't work), I heard my mother say this to Aunt Harriet:

"You think you've got troubles? Pamela's a women's libber."

Well!

I took it as a supreme compliment.

She was afraid I'd burn my bra, I guess. She needn't have worried: it had taken me way too long to fill it to fling it into a political bonfire.

In fact, the revolution was under way from the neck up. That's really why my mother, in the saying of the day, was having a cow.

New ideas were taking hold in my head like the Dippity-Doo on it. When my chums and I weren't sitting around Susie Levitan's bedroom laughing ourselves silly, playing bridge, or eating Susie's fabulous cheese soufflé, salad and chocolate mousse on Saturday nights, we discussed the issues of the day. Specifically, the Vietnam War and women's liberation.

I am eternally mortified that I was one of those "Fine Young People" who worked to reelect that *CREEP*-y president in '72, but at the time it was a highly parental-approved political and social activity. Plus, I liked the energy and what I thought was the importance of being on the winning team. I'd just come from three years of junior high school, where I was the last to get picked for *any* team and then played so badly I wished I'd been pilloried outright, so what could be more heady than working, however many ignorances removed, for the president himself? (Years later, when I met George McGovern as a journalist, I felt like Homer Simpson: *"D'oh!"*)

Today peer pressure can lead to body piercing; back then it led to mind piercing. One year into Nixon's second term, my more politically sophisticated friends were doing their best with me, a Republican daughter. (My parents were selective when it came to deriding "peer pressure": on the one hand, they exhorted me not to "follow the crowd" when it came to censuring Nixon and the Vietnam War; on the other hand, they were all for it when it came to aiming for Ivy League colleges.)

On women's lib, though, my girl—women—friends and I were in complete agreement from the movement's get-go. In fact, we were flabbergasted that there were actually people who believed women couldn't or shouldn't do anything men did and get paid equally for it. This is what women's lib meant to us. The problem was that most people were arguing that women's lib meant men shouldn't open doors for women and that ladies' rooms would give way to unisex bathrooms with urinals. I think women's lib generated more dumb discussions in the early '70s than just about any other subject except, Is Paul Dead.

We had no idea at the time that women's lib was taking place in Susie's bedroom, that when a group of women of any age get together to fervently share ideas, hopes and plans about being women and being proud of it, that's how feminism takes root. We learned from you that the personal is political, but for those of us who were introduced to women's lib via media disdain, parental put-downs and heated debates with the boys in our English classes, it was the political that became personal. We realized women's lib was about *us* and that what happened (or didn't happen) because of it would affect the rest of our lives. I can't fathom now how we knew this in high school, but we did. Some of our teachers stayed "Miss" long after we'd adopted "Ms."

I keep referring to the women's movement as women's lib here in part because the term "feminism" came later, but also because "women's lib" more accurately describes its early shouts for and about freedom. Somehow we got to know the truth tellings of Betty Friedan, Simone de Beauvoir, and Germaine Greer. A *TIME Magazine* article introduced me to the artist Judy Chicago. The music of Joni Mitchell, Laura Nyro and Janis Ian floated down to us from older sisters' bedrooms. When I wasn't with Sue, Dolly, Robin and Linney, I was with my friends Beth, Madeline, and Beverly, listening to Carly Simon and Carole King records over and over, especially *No Secrets* and *Tapestry*. Joni, Laura, Janis, Carly and Carole—the quintet who scored for us first the revolution, then the revelation: women were writing, playing and singing *their own* words and music. We loved them. The part in "Waited So Long" when James Taylor sings after Carly, "She's no virgin," still makes me feel irrepressibly happy.

I can't remember when I first knew who you were, but I know it was before *Ms.* magazine came on the scene. I used to read your stories in *New York* magazine when I babysat in junior high. Baby-sitting was great for expanding the mind. Until then I thought all fathers got only *TIME, Newsweek, National Geographic,* and the *Far East Economic* and *Columbia Journalism Reviews.* Thanks to baby-sitting, I knew every *Playboy* cartoon from the past seven years. Personally, I owe a huge thank you to *Playboy* for publishing the great Jean Shepherd's short stories, but it's a mark of my deepest respect for you that *Ms.,* when I discovered it, became my top sneak read. (Loved your *New York* Playboy Bunny story, by the way.)

I wanted to write you this letter because women's lib–turned–feminism has left a huge, deep and joyous imprint on my life, and you, more than anyone, are the personality in it who has stood out to me. I've read that in the early days of the movement, you were terrified of public speaking, but from the first, everything about you shouted confidence to me. You and your sisters made me believe two things in my heart: that the working world would welcome me and that I was lucky—both for my dreams' sake and for the sheer fun of it—to have been born a woman this time around.

As serious and important as women's lib was (is), and as angry as it could be, you all always looked like you were having a great time. You yourself looked as bold as what you had to say in those aviators and boots! What a sense of freedom and exhilaration you conveyed. It was that exhilaration—with life, with purpose, with possibilities—that inspired me and so many other women I know to delight in who we were and plan to succeed at what we could be.

How can I thank you for urging me by both your words and your actions to recognize and cherish my membership in this great and powerful club?

It's true that I love men, but it will always be a love of the Other. My love for women is based on the warmth of our familiarity and the simplicity of our sameness. With men my love is the intrigue of discovery and the complexity of otherness. In one club I'm a conspiratorial insider; in the other, a sly outsider. I belong to the club of women, and I infiltrate the club of men—I've got a great deal going here!

If it hadn't been for you, the face and voice of women's lib/feminism to me, I don't know that I would have had the pride and confidence I've had. I know I wouldn't have had the opportunities. As it is, I've never felt shut out from any experience in life, and for that I thank you and all the "libbers" with the deepest appreciation and gratitude.

So let me tell you what happened to my mother once she got over her shock that I was a women's libber, an acceptance—or resignation—by the way, that took years. She may read *Cathy* cartoons because she identifies with Cathy's mother, but my mom did have a *click!* of sorts. Only it dawned in the form of an "Uh-oh." The chasm between us that gaped at the start of my college years—ME: Smith = Gloria Steinem's school; HER: Smith = Julie Nixon's school—narrowed quite suddenly in March 1976, when my father died and she had to go to work. She was forty-two.

For years she was underpaid, and her mind was underutilized in various jobs. In her first job after she was widowed, at a start-up company, she developed a strategic marketing plan that, incidentally, would have saved the company good money. After reading it, her male boss called her into his office, slammed the fifteen-page sheaf of carefully typed pages down on his desk and roared, *"You're a secretary trying to get out of a job, and if I ever see you on the phone again on a personal call, you'll be fired!"* My mother was never one for a "Fuck you, asshole," and she just didn't know the tactful, professional version of it: "I admire your swift decision-making abilities, but why don't you just sit on this one for a while?" So she sobbed. In his office. A friend of hers (male) told her she had the makings of a lawsuit, but my mother truly believed no one would give her a job ever again if she pursued it, and she had a family to support.

Eventually my mother landed some great jobs—she's a crack researcher—but she remained woefully underpaid, because she'd undersold herself in that first job and was never able to catch up.

Had my mother, with her lightning-quick mind and cleverness, been born in my generation and into a different family, she almost certainly would have gone to law school, and in fact she briefly considered it when she was in her fifties. But then she discovered, by way of a part-time sales job at a store that sold reproductions of historical artifacts, that she was brilliant at developing gift ideas. At sixty, my mother started her own historical gifts business. She's doing *great!* I'm so proud of her! She belongs to a Virginia professional women's network—a group, she says, that "gives you courage when you see what other women have done."

A proud moment in 1997: My mother had just turned sixty-four. It was a warm August day. She was on the phone with me. When she answered the phone, I heard my stepfather yell, *"Who is it?"* and she yelled back, *"Pamela."*

It had never before occurred to me to ask her what I wanted to know. What, I asked her now, did she think of feminism? Had it affected her life at all?

"I'm not a feminist," my mother answered. "Whoever said a woman can have it all made it harder for women—the baby doesn't suffer, but the mother does; she's always tired. Unless she has a *lot* of money.

"The feminists were right about the money. I got started too late to know about the money. When I went to work, all I knew was how to please men. I never asked for enough money. I thought that the men making five times as much money as I was were five times as smart as me. . . . I didn't realize you should be compensated for the value of the work you did. I wasn't a success in the business world, and if my daughters are honest, they know that they didn't learn anything about succeeding in it from me—I'm not a fighter."

Feminists, my mother told me, are fighters. Then she added—with no prompting on my part, I swear—"A fighter is someone like Gloria Steinem.

"Gloria Steinem fought for the rights of women, fought to make a woman equal to a man," my mother said. "She had credibility, because she wasn't saying, 'Go kill men!'; she just encouraged women to do their best. I admire her for that, for getting up there and saying that a woman should do whatever she feels she does the best.

"I didn't believe that before women's lib. I remember once having to see a woman breast surgeon in New York. It was Christmas; only the woman was on call. I went in thinking, What kind of business is this, for a woman to be a breast surgeon? Then I realized—she had breasts! And she was *good*. One of the best in New York. She fought for equal pay for the women doctors at her hospital, and she won—it was in all the papers.

"But I still believe—I *know* this—that men and women are different. Women are more flexible; they put up with more crap. Women are more sensitive than men. They have a better sense about people. They're more vulnerable.

"I don't know that much about Gloria Steinem, but what I liked about her was that she was a fighter who still seemed vulnerable at times. Like a . . . woman."

Of course I wish, as a post-Watergate journalist, that my mother didn't still believe it was the press that did Nixon in, but what can you do?

Gloria, I feel so lucky that, as Janis Ian sang it, I learned the truth at seventeen. Your convictions and your courage in writing and speaking them have enriched millions of lives beyond measure. Mine is one of them.

Thank you.

Sincerely,

Pam Janis

"*Warm summer breeze blows endlessly,*
Touching the hearts of those who feel
One summer dream. . . ."
—ELECTRIC LIGHT ORCHESTRA

Dear Mr. Rumsey, Sir,

Some people acquire a second family by marrying into one. I roommated into mine.

I'm writing to thank you for welcoming me into your family almost as soon, it seems, as Smith College sent me the letter informing me that my freshman-year roommate would be one Mary C. Rumsey, of Berkeley, California. Had I known then that that name would hold half my life's history, I might not have immediately written your daughter a letter wondering, among other things, whether she was a blonde and her dad was a Hollywood movie producer. (Well, that's what California meant to me. My parents, who could only read as far as "Berkeley," wondered whether Mary was a "radical" who would lead student uprisings, sleep in the nude and know where Patty Hearst was.)

Okay, so you were in the book business, and my raven-haired friend could have grown up in Greenwich for all she knew from radical. Which is, as it turns out, where Patty Hearst lives now.

Who could have foreseen that the Rumsey family would radicalize my life in ways I'm grateful for every single day of it?

I wish I'd written you this letter while you were still alive. Somehow, even though my own dad died suddenly during sophomore year, it never occurred to me afterward that *you* wouldn't be around to walk me down the aisle, should the day ever come. It's been almost two years now since you left, during the last week in April, a week so unseasonably hot in the Bay Area that everyone who came to say good-bye to you remarked on it, knowing how much you hated the cold.

I still want you to know how much your kindness, affection and generosity of spirit—as well as your wonderful family: Julie, Mary, Schuyler, Peter and John—have meant to me.

You know, I never asked you and Julie this: who did *you* worry Mary had drawn in Smith's roommate roulette? Someone who was so hopelessly bad in math that she'd screw up every dominoes game she ever played with you even when you reminded her how to play at the start of each one?

Glad I didn't disappoint you.

The first time I met Mary's entire family was after a huge weeks-long fight with my parents.

It was just after freshman year had ended. My roomie—who I still call Roommate or Rums, my nickname for her, and who still calls me Roommate or Jan, her nickname for me (I think we're the only two people who call each other those things, like cats who reserve that special chirping sound for their person)—had invited me to visit her family in Berkeley that summer.

Yippee!! I was finally going to get to see that mythical land of the Beach Boys, CALIFORNIA! I was so excited, as Rums would say, I could hardly stand it. Not only that, but a visit between school years would neatly solve the problem my roommate and I had quickly realized we'd have over the summer: not being able to talk every single day and night.

There were only two problems: the pills who were my parents. My father didn't want me to go because he was my father. My mother didn't want me to go because my father said so. It was that kind of discussion.

I'd never wanted anything more in my life, it seemed, than to visit the Rumseys in California. Mary and I ran up huge phone bills in June discussing the matter, but my parents were immovable. I started to think evil thoughts: "It's because they're not Jewish."

"That's *nonsense!*," my father roared at me. "*I don't know who Mary Rumsey's parents are! I don't know what kind of supervision you'd have! I don't know how you expect to get a job and earn money this summer!* Pishers *don't make the rules in this house,* I *do! The answer is* no!"

When Mary told you and Julie what was going on in Stamford's Yiddish Theatre, the two of you placed a call to Howard and Lucille.

"George Rumsey sounds like a reasonable man," my father announced to me afterward, my mother interrupting him with "Julie's lovely—just lovely."

"I expect you to be on your best behavior at all times and to obey every word he says."

Julie, Mary and the boys can correct me if I'm wrong, but I think telling everyone about my dad's strict orders to mind you like a drill sergeant was how the thing about my calling you "Sir" got started.

How can I begin to thank you for that reassuring phone call to my fearful parents? Because in that conversation you didn't just say all the right dad-to-dad things about the strict supervision of college girls' hours and activities; you told my parents (and me) I *would* have a job and earn money that summer, a job in California shelving books with Rums in your book warehouse in Oakland.

Bless you, Mr. Rumsey, Sir.

That July into August, you and your family presented
me with the exquisitely wrapped gift of Northern
California, then watched as I opened it, layer by lush layer.
It was as though you and Julie planned my nineteenth
summer like a party.

First there were the sights that I couldn't believe you
saw every day just by waking up: the tall palms that
curved along the Uplands; the lemons growing on a tree in
your own backyard; the reflector lane lights on California
freeways; the cooled stucco houses like your own.

The trip started with a trip. On the way to pick up
your second son, Peter, at Boy Scout camp at Big Bear
Mountain, we drove through tiny mountain towns on
winding roads, sunlight entwined in shadowy pines, rock
and valley vistas around every twist of the asphalt ribbon.
We stopped for ice cream in a high hamlet as old as the
gold rush, a way stop so remote that finding an ice cream
cone there couldn't have been more surprising if we'd
stopped to ask graybeards in tatters with picks and pans
where we could get one. Thanks for treating me to the
best strawberry ice cream cone I've had in my life, Mr.
Rumsey, Sir, the frozen, tangy wild berries priceless
nuggets themselves.

You teased Rums and me (by then you were calling me
"Pammy baby") that whole trip about how we never
stopped talking. (But let me just point out here that your
lovely daughter, dark and deep as Frost's woods on a
snowy evening, wrote her senior thesis on the concept of
silence. Of course, we talked about that too.)

At Big Bear Mountain, we met up with a jamboree of
Boy Scouts and family members. The sky above the

campfire dinner and sing-along that night was my first starry California mountain sky, a sky like none I'd seen before, the darkness darker and the stars brighter than a Connecticut winter solstice. Standing among the picnic totes beforehand, drinking white wine in cooler-chilled glasses, tall white-haired Uncle Dick Hafner, who was to become a special friend to me that summer with his journalism background and kind interest in mine, told me, "It *is* a good life, out here."

I could see that all around me. There was something else I was seeing, too: an extended family that treated each and every member, regardless of age, with interest, kindness and respect.

Thank you for making me feel like an honorary and honored daughter of yours, George. That summer, your family showed me, in the way they related to one another, how I wanted to be. You all made me mindful of how important it is to people of all ages, abilities and kinds to feel significant before they can feel—or be—their best. I watched and took mental notes from you for more than twenty years, beginning that summer, and I only hope I learned as well as your own children did.

Back in Berkeley after a glorious week at the family cabin on Lake Tahoe, gorgeous days drifted one into the next. Rums and I went to work with you every day (Julie packed us all lunch), carting and sorting hundreds of thousands of books, it seemed, that you'd bought at auctions, ordered or otherwise found. In the late afternoons and on weekends, we sometimes headed to "the Ranch," the family pool in Lafayette, for picnic dinners and swimming.

All that summer, relatives and out-of-town friends of
the Rumsey kids and Hafner cousins came and went like
the Bay tides; we never knew who was going to be at the
Ranch or on your redwood deck, sipping California wine
and munching hors d'oeuvres after work. You presided
both at the warehouse and after hours with that
combination of easy graciousness and keen attentiveness
that was so *you*. I'm still trying to capture your style of
working really hard, then relaxing effortlessly.

I learned from you what a gift it is to be firmly planted
in every moment you experience so as not to miss it.
Sometimes when I'm having a Total Chaos day—three
deadlines, a laundry pileup, no time to return phone
messages, a race to FedEx before it closes—I think of the
unperturbed way you did everything from bidding on
books to raising children. I wanted so much to be like
you, calm and lively at the same time, attending to the
business or pleasure at hand seemingly with time for
everything and everyone and without stress. I hate to tell
you this, Mr. Rumsey, Sir, but after twenty-four years I've
had to conclude that my genes overpower your example.

You're still my gold standard for an even-keeled life,
though, however long it eludes me.

Whenever you promised that the summer's visitors
would have "piles of fun" doing something, we knew an
adventure was waiting for us. What didn't we see and do?
We walked into the wind across the Golden Gate Bridge;
strolled Sausalito; checked out a fortune cookie factory in a
Chinatown alley; ascended Coit Tower; twisted down
Lombard Street; hung on cable cars; wandered Fishermen's
Wharf and the Cannery; shopped Union Square; picnicked

at Golden Gate Park; explored Inverness and Point Reyes; wine-tasted Napa Valley; and lunched demurely at Mary's dear Grandmother's ladies-only social club in the city. But somehow we always ended up back on the redwood deck with the French street sign, *Rue de Monbel,* from the years you took the whole family to live in Paris, the late-'60s Berkeley-campus unrest years.

About the only Bay Area experience you guys *didn't* give me that summer was an earthquake.

I am so grateful to you and your family for opening the jewel case that is San Francisco to me, along with the mountains and Lake Tahoe. What forever wonders I first saw with you! You, Sir, may have had the movable feast of Paris from your Marshall Plan days as a young man there for the rest of *your* life, but *I* have the salad bar of California.

The day I had to leave, the lovely Julie (still then, to me, Mrs. Rumsey) presented me with a parting remembrance that made me cry when she gave it to me and still does when I think of it. Thank you from the bottom of my East Coast, supermarket-produce heart, Julie, for that gift, the sweetest of tart delights: the little lemon tree. I'm sure you knew it wouldn't survive its first New England winter, but I understood its message perfectly, and my heart soared.

I went back east a Christmas-dazzled child, a Californian in spirit and soul. I'm still playing at being semi-bicoastal, but Northern California is my heart's haven, and I always realize it anew when I return to it. That's why I wanted to write you this letter here, in California, where you embraced me into your family. Thank you for the eternal gift of helping my soul find its way home.

*　　*　　*

You honored me with as many kindnesses in the twenty-one years of your lifetime that followed that summer as there were books in your warehouse.

Thank you for the twin pairs of toe socks from Carmel that you sent Rums and me that fall—for the cold, you and Julie wrote, but we knew the real reason, because we missed you both too.

Thank you for flying to Columbus to visit me at Kenyon the next semester, soon after my dad died, knowing two things: 1) I still needed a father, and 2) I missed Rums (the only reason not to have transferred from Smith) terribly. You came, you said, to "check on" your store at Ohio State, but thanks for coming to check on me too. I can't believe you endured a night in my girls' dorm and a MAN IN SHOWER sign on the hall bathroom door. You even flew Rums in, too, for a surprise visit the next day, knowing we'd talk all night.

When I lived in New York after college, there you were, too, taking my friend Vicki and me out to dinner at a Village place that was piles of fun, urging us to order the lobster. (Thanks, we did.)

I've always marveled at the irrepressible way you enjoyed life and how you made yourself at home anywhere you found—or put—yourself, warmly drawing whoever happened to be there toward you instantly. Raised by an aunt in Rockford, Illinois, you moved between worlds and people so easily from tough beginnings. You were such a living lesson that early losses can make you form even stronger attachments in life, stronger because when you create them yourself, you treasure them all the more. You never missed that Rumsey tradition, Sunday-night supper, with your family. (Julie says once, when an odd social conflict occurred, the two of you stayed at some party for about ten minutes, then you said, "C'mon, let's go home and see what the kids are doing.")

Thanks for showing all of us not to take the families we do have for granted.

The one time I can remember you ever saying anything about your tough childhood was in a phone call to my brother, an eleven-year-old you'd never met, right after our dad died. That happened to me too, you told him. It doesn't mean you won't grow up and have a happy life.

And it was clear you were happiest with Julie, the love of your life (she was part of the movable feast you took from Paris), Mary, Schuyler, Peter and John.

Well. So, you weren't a movie producer, but I do want to thank you for producing Mary C. Rumsey. Our conversations meander on, thanks especially to Jim Dorskind, who moved his wife to Washington, D.C. Which is where I saw you for the last time, at Rums's fortieth birthday party, in her and Jim's living room less than two months before your stroke.

"Hey, Pammy baby," you said as I was getting ready to leave the evening's piles of fun, "hurry up . . . get married. I don't have forever."

Oh, how I wish you had, Mr. Rumsey, Sir.

To me you will always be the embodiment of our shared adopted state, California: as expansive as its skies, solid as its mountains, generous as its valleys, deep as its waters, warm as its sunshine, twinkly as the night lights of its chief northern city seen from across the bay.

Thank you for being all these things to everyone who

knew and loved you while you were with us and misses you now, especially the woman you first met as Mary's roommate, one Pamela R. Janis from Stamford, Connecticut.

With my deepest love and gratitude,

Pammy baby

Dear Mary, Suzanne, and Cindi,

You guys were my dearest Smith chums, and I'm so glad our friendships continue to this day.

Mary (Rums): Reducing our years of friendship to thanking you for being my roommate seems as ridiculous as how we spent our last night at Smith together, you in a sleeping bag on the floor of my senior-year single (especially ridiculous considering we had adjoining rooms, connected by the bathroom with the claw-foot tub where we took turns drawing each other baths because we liked the way that sounded).

So thank you, first, for being my roommate, but then for all the experiences we've shared since.

Thank you for introducing me to California and for taking me to my very first manicure there when we were twenty-one (how had I lived so long without being queried, "Square or oval?").

Thank you for all the fabulous meals you've made for me in Northampton, Berkeley and Washington . . . for making me part of first the Rumsey and then the Dorskind families . . . for loving seraphs and cherubs as much as I do and for giving me that special birthday angel who watches over me when I sleep.

Thank you for all the birthdays we've shared, for the parties you've given and for making me a bridesmaid at your and Jim's wedding. Thanks, too, for making me functional at Suzanne's wedding the summer carpal tunnel crippled me and you spent that weekend zipping up my party dresses, conveying plates of food from buffet lines to me, and carting me all over Chicago from one event to the next. (With Jim on crutches from that waterskiing mishap, boy, were we two a sorry song.)

Thank you, Rums, for so many things, and this most of all: for being on the train from Northampton the day my dad died. We stood together on the Stamford station platform, holding each other, unable to speak, then you said the words that said so much more: "I came to cook dinner."

What is friendship but the marking of passages together?

Suzanne: The first few weeks of school, before anyone really knew anyone, you were giving all the fourth-floor Martha Wilson girls the Juicyfruit gum that your Wrigley's dad had sent, and it didn't take long for everyone to know who you were. Thanks for being probably the friendliest person I've ever met—that's as true two-and-a-half decades later as it was in September 1974. Thank you for the openness and common sense you bring to my life, no matter how many months separate our note cards, and for being a decisive woman who knows exactly who she is I've tried to learn from you.

Also, thanks for making the expression "We had a blast" a permanent part of my lexicon. And we especially did have a blast that fantastic week a few summers ago when Peter was still in Chicago and we were glued to the Menendez brothers trial on Court TV when we weren't running around Venice and Santa Monica.

Thanks for having me as a houseguest then and for always making the years melt away.

Cindi: Thank you for teaching me how to cross-country ski the night our eighty-eight housemates kicked us out because they were having a mixer and we hadn't paid our social dues. I remember falling near the lake and not being able to stand up, finally just surrendering to the frozen ground, both of us in hysterics. But I've mastered the sport since, and it's one of my favorites. I think of you every time I snap my boots into my skis. And fall in the snow.

Thank you, too, for sharing your lovely parents, Dr. John and Esty Duff (and the seven sibs), and for welcoming me home to Oakmarsh. I love the way you still use your experience of growing up in a big family to always seek out what's unique about an individual and embrace them as special, as an "only child." You valued diversity and multiculturalism in your life and friendships decades before the words took on a political connotation.

Thank you for your always open mind and heart to all of God's creations.

Thanks, Smith, for bringing these forever friends into my life!

Love,

Pam

Dear Kim,

I miss the days we laughed our heads off at Smith and also in New York afterward. You were the one who introduced me to the Eagles and ELO, also, through a party invitation, to my graduate-school beau.

There are many things I could thank you for from the time we were living on a series of *Seinfeld* sets, but there's one thing you did in college that meant the world to me at the time and still does.

When my dad died sophomore year, you wrote me a beautiful sympathy note, which I still have. You wrote that even though you didn't know my dad, he must have been very special to have fathered me. That still makes me cry.

Thank you for always saying just the right thing.

Thanks, too, for what I thought was a great Kim line. It wasn't until our tenth reunion that I found out you stole it from Bob Hope, but I, too, "hope you never die."

Love,

Pam J.

Dear Penny,

I don't know that "Thank you" can ever convey my gratitude to you or that there could be enough thank-yous to express how I feel when I think of you, my first professional editor. I owe you so much! You launched me as a professional writer, helped enlarge and refine my career in its earliest years, and always cheered me on.

Wow, I never thought when we first met—I was eighteen and you were thirty-five!—that I'd ever get to a point when I'd be measuring my career in years rather than dreams.

When your first letter to me arrived in the mail one summer day after freshman year in 1975, I looked at the printed return address with the *Seventeen* magazine logo for what seemed an eternity before I tore it open. Why so eagerly, I'll never know—I was poised for a rejection, expecting to officially feel disapppointed after weeks of vain hopes, getting ready to pretend to my hovering mother that I didn't really care.

Instead, your friendly letter informed me that you'd accepted my story about what it was like to not be asked to my high school senior prom. (I'd retell it here to refresh your memory if it wouldn't have the dismaying effect of also refreshing mine. Anyway, this is the gist of it: no one asked me to my senior-class prom, and at some point in my misery and humilation—misery at not having been asked, humiliation at having been turned down by the *two* boys I begged—I realized: "Hey, this is pretty funny.")

I'll never forget your kindness and congratulations in that letter. I couldn't believe, first, that *Seventeen* had accepted the story, and second, that an obviously important but very nice-sounding *editor*—an editor whose name, Penny Post, was on the masthead—had written me a warm, personal letter praising it. I realize now how truly extraordinary you were as an editor and mentor to young writers; you made every story you edited feel like a collaboration between colleagues.

The best part of your letter was actually a criticism of the story: you suggested in a helpful way that its ending was a little harsh (it was some diatribe against my mother for making the prom seem so important, I think). Instead, you wrote, "Why not . . . ?" and then proposed such an easy, clear and positive way to improve the ending that I instantly saw how much better the whole story would be. Having never had an editor before, I couldn't have realized at the time how gifted you were, but I know now. You made it seem as though you weren't just editing a story; you were *celebrating* it with the writer.

I remember how nervous I was the first time I called you when I was reworking the story and how good your welcoming voice made me feel. You invited me to New York to have lunch with you: I took the train into New York, and, sitting in *Seventeen*'s reception area, I saw a tall, lanky, energetic woman with light blue eyes and hair the color of wheat, her face creased in what looked to be a permanent smile, striding through the hall. I bet that's Penny Post, I thought.

It *was* you. When you came out to greet me, I felt like I'd met my guardian angel in the guise of a teen-magazine articles editor.

The mag, by the way, paid me $350 for that first story, but even more thrilling than the check was putting my signature on the *Seventeen* contract in triplicate: white, yellow and pink copies.

More thrilling still was the story's actual publication in *Seventeen*'s March 1976 issue. My journalist dad died suddenly, one week after my first professional byline appeared in it. So I'm indebted to you on that score too.

But I have so much else to thank you for too!

As our friendship blossomed (and I grew older while you only seemed to grow younger), you continued to be my guardian angel. It was you who told me about and encouraged me to apply for an American Society of Magazine Editors internship between junior and senior years, which led me to a joyful summer at *Advertising Age*. You supported my J-school application, then told me to look up a young L.A. reporter friend of yours in my class, Jeff Gottlieb, who became a friend for life. (You'll love this: Jeff and I have a standing pact that if neither of us is married in 1999, we'll be each other's New Year's Eve date for the millennium. It's not the match you hoped for, but we're committed in our own "So, anything *new*?" way.)

Do you remember when you first moved to L.A. in the late '70s, you were clearing out your West Side apartment and told me to take anything I wanted that you'd otherwise trash? I took your heavy, plastic-covered San Francisco kitchen wall poster, having just begun my love affair with San Francisco a few summers earlier. Do you believe, Penny, that for twenty years I've carted that thing everywhere I've lived? Since you last saw it, it's hung in seven apartment kitchens in three states. It's always the first thing of mine to go up in a new place, the thing for me that says "home."

Thank you for the poster and the memories of you that

hang with it—our great times in New York and L.A., the striking clothes you sewed and wore, the peach tree behind your first California house in Santa Monica, the chicken mole you made one night when I was there and the moving poetry, letters, and stories of yours that you shared with me.

I'm more than grateful to you for starting my career in *Seventeen* at eighteen, Penny. You will always hold the dearest of places in my heart for welcoming me so generously and instructively into the ranks of the published.

Thank you for making me *glad* no one asked me to my prom.

Love,

Pam

Dear Julie, Nancy, and Paul,

Three semesters at Kenyon were all it took to ensure
that I'd laugh for the rest of my life, and not just at the
memories. Thanks to you guys and Vicki, my dad's
forbidding me to transfer anywhere else turned out to be
the luckiest edict of my life. I cried and yelled because I
couldn't go to school in California. Fact: soulmates always
meet up, even if they don't come quietly.

With you, Julie, I first unleashed my woman's wild side,
the part that would run with the wolves if it could keep
up. One night junior year we stayed up so late talking
about the usual things—Nietzsche, D. H. Lawrence,
Simone De Beauvoir, Song of Songs, *Even Cowgirls Get the
Blues*, the two guys who lived down the hall, and
bleaching vs. depilatories—that we just *had* to see the sun
rise. We raced out of the dorm, only to discover a low-
lying fog obscuring the eastern horizon. You ran into and
through it yelling, *"Women! Mothers! Daughters! Sisters!"* and
I fell behind, laughing in the mist but stumbling along
still, because I wanted to be like you, Italian warrior
goddess that you were. Are. Who else would drive another
lawyer to make faces at her during a deposition and then
say, "Let the record reflect that opposing counsel stuck his
tongue out at me"? Thanks, Jules, for being my "take no
crap" role model in life.

Nancy, from you I've learned that wonderful things
can start with one word: "Hello." Our paths might never
have crossed if they hadn't literally collided. We met
face-to-face coming from opposite directions on a single-
file path cleared in the snow one late January day when

I'd been at Kenyon less than a week. We both started to laugh at our traffic predicament, then you gave me the widest, friendliest smile I'd ever seen and said, "Hello, I'm Nancy Bolotin." Meeting you that way has always made me wonder how many friendships in life we miss by hurrying past. Thank you, Nance, for stopping. Okay, so you had no choice—our two roads converged—but you didn't have to say "Hello." And that has made all the difference.

Thanks to Paul, I know that Someone is playing with a universe-sized chemistry set, doing experiments in His galactic bedroom just to see what will happen. Running out of gas on a moonless, subzero February night on our way to pick Vicki up at the airport and having to walk miles to a house guarded by killer dogs was typical of the cosmic KABOOM that always happens when our karmas commingle. I borrowed your astronomy notes—we both got Ds. We put in a much-anticipated road-trip audiocassette, hit PLAY on the tapedeck—a new one—and it was the day the music died when it jammed. No matter how old we get, we're what would happen if you rigged jumper cables the wrong way. But I'll never miss a meal you've cooked or take down the woodcut from your art major days that hangs in my living room. And thanks, too, Grimes, for the tip to polish patent leather with Vaseline.

It's inconceivable that I could have missed meeting all of you in life, that I ever could have transferred to another school. So, clearly, there's no such thing as "could have." For the profundity and profanity we've shared all these years—even as we headed toward school in Julie's mommy van, with the tapedeck Grimes and I broke, for our twentieth reunion—thanks, soulmates.

Love,

That new woman from Smith

Dear President Carter,

Thank you for being as compassionate as you are and for having the faith you do—in people, in the notion that politics is a means to do good in our country and our world and in the processes that can, and sometimes do, lead to peace.

I've admired you since the 1976 presidential election, the first I voted in. Casting my ballot for you (absentee; I was away at school) was a proud moment of citizenship for me.

I will tell you this frankly: I couldn't care less about both the Democratic and Republican parties. I don't see true across-the-board principles in either case; gray areas, like self-interest, abound on both sides.

So what I learned from you as our president wasn't so much political as it was . . . human. What your presidency underscored for me is that only a peaceful person, a person at peace with him- or herself, can be a broker of it in the larger community. The current restless, conflict-loving, Congress-as-schoolyard political adolescents give me the willies: who wants to elect someone desperately searching to fill all the holes in their heart at citizen expense?

What I've always admired about you, President Carter, is that you don't seem to confuse advocacy with mindfulness, or self-restraint with humility. In other words, the political with the spiritual. And thank you for knowing—and showing—that the tenets of faith don't belong to just one religion.

Thank you for your four years as my president and

all the work you've done since to build peace and good in the world for its people as surely as you've built them homes.

Sincerely,

Pam Janis

Dear Mark,

I know you're married and have a family, but I hope it's okay to write to one of my first and all-time greatest boyfriends. (Or is this like your worst nightmare—an ex-girlfriend who's a writer?)

Don't worry: it's a *thank-you* note.

Hi, Laurie. I don't know what he's told you about his Kenyon College sweetheart, but he wrote me the most beautiful letter about you when he met you in Senegal, working for the Peace Corps. I cried when I got it, not because he was marrying someone else but because he was so in love with you and so happy that you'd married him. It wasn't the kind of letter you want to find among the MasterCard offers and Lands' End catalogues in your mailbox every day, but I was—and am—thrilled that my long-ago love found the woman of his dreams.

The reason I'm writing now, Mark, is that I wanted to thank you for a wonderful couple of years back in the Stoned Age. *We grow old, we grow old, we shall wear our joints rolled.* Who said that? Oh, I'm sorry; you have kids. So, for the record, kids: that was just a line to make your dad—who did *not* do drugs, which was only one of the reasons I liked him—laugh. As you know by now, he's a pretty funny guy, and he always cracked me up with little verbal surprises like that. (Tell me he's not still peering through his fingers in Chinese restaurants, saying, "Peeking duck?" Then ask him to tell you about the time my mother carried a sizzling platter into the dining room, announcing, "Duck, everybody," and he did.)

But to thank you, Mark, just for making me laugh so hard I'd start coughing, wouldn't really convey how grateful I've felt to you over the twenty-something years since. I can't think of my father's death without thinking of you, too: how you were with me when the news came over the phone; how you called Nancy Bolotin, the friend who'd introduced us, to come over to my dorm room, too; how you tenderly helped me pack and sped me to the Columbus airport in the car you named the Red Wind; how you drove the eleven hours from your hometown of Asheville, North Carolina, to Stamford during spring break the next week to be with me and my family, whom you hadn't even met yet.

We'd been going out all of three weeks.

We were inseparable that whole semester, my first and your last at Kenyon. (That got extremely complicated, given that we both had roommates.) I couldn't believe you didn't freak out or run when my dad's death interrupted our so-sweet courtship—or that it continued to unfold back at school afterward in a way that I still marvel at for its simple happiness.

I'm grateful for the memories I have of that short time we had to enjoy on campus together before you graduated. We took long, long walks during a strange and sudden thaw that winter that confused every seed and bulb in Ohio. We had a standing Wednesday-night cream-of-mushroom Cup-A-Soup date after my American Lit seminar. On spring weekends, we cruised around Knox County in the Red Wind, searching out rustic knolls to loll in and ignore the looming question, What Happens After Graduation? I remember so many odd details that made us Us: how even though I loved watching the Oscars, we didn't; how we listened to Jesse Colin Young's music in your room; how we'd just lose it every time some song

about a dead dog named Shannon came on the radio in
mine. It's such a grab bag of scenes and memories that
don't resemble anyone else's sweetheart serenade but at the
same time resemble everyone's: there's nothing *bad* in that
bag, nothing we don't want to remember, nothing we don't
cherish.

One night you came over after studying in the library
and announced you'd just found the perfect definition of
our relationship in *Don Juan*: "Affection, desire and the
intellect." Oh, sigh.

Commencement and the summer came—on the same
day, it seemed—and we continued our romance in
Stamford and Asheville.

(My sisters and brother and I still have our favorite
Mark Ames stories from that summer. One is the time we
were all eating steak and you picked yours up and barked
at it, explaining that your grandfather always used to say,
"It always tastes better if you growl at it." We all thank
you for that one.)

Thank you for showing me your hometown and for
introducing me to all the people who were dear to you
before me. Your mom and sister welcomed me so warmly;
I lost touch with them at some point after you got
married, because I felt that was right, given Laurie's place
in your family, but I've never forgotten their kindness. I
thank them, too, for accepting me as your girlfriend when
they'd hardly have you to themselves before you were
headed off to the Peace Corps, to Ghana, that September
that came too soon.

Fortunately, you were a great letter writer.

Thanks for all the wonderful if somewhat erratically
delivered letters, photos and poems from West Africa.

Sometimes I'd get nothing for two weeks, then three thick envelopes would arrive the same day. You were so great about sharing every detail and discovery with me as you helped care for Ghana's children by building them schools.

And thank you for taking that wild Air Ghana ride to meet me in Paris Christmas my senior year back at Smith (the plane trip that took off a day late and then took you only as far as London because the pilot decided in midair that's where he felt like going).

I can't be in Paris today without remembering how you called my attention to the way the late-afternoon light and shadow plays with the curves of certain streets in the eighteenth arrondissement, and then noticing it anew. Or remembering the magic of the one night we stayed at the Ritz.

I know we broke up officially that spring—it would have been sooner if the mail to and from Africa had been speedier—but I'm so glad we stayed friends afterward for as long as we did. And we did, me in New York, then New Jersey and Washington; you back in North Carolina, then Senegal. There's been so much news I've wanted to catch you up on over the years. . . .

One thing I always loved about our relationship was the way we constantly traded information—news, confidences, jokes, gossip; things people said in class, along Middle Path, or in the Pierce and Gund dining halls; interesting stuff in the newspaper. Did we ever stop talking and laughing together? Before I met you, I had my best conversations with women and assumed that male–female relationships were different, that I couldn't hope or expect to find a talker like me. Thanks to you, I know what's missing now if I don't. You showed me how great conversation could make every day of a relationship both important and entertaining, especially if the guy you were talking with was your best friend.

Affection, desire and the intellect.

Thank you for all of it, Mark, all the fun, and all the memories. Thank you for the empathy and compassion that impelled you to cross oceans, borders and cultures to help people. Thank you especially for being there for me through the toughest of times. Thank you for waking me up on my twentieth birthday with strawberries and champagne.

Your family is blessed to have you, and I wish you, Laurie, and all of you the best, always.

Love,

Pam

Dear Madame Ritz,

Some years ago, while your family still owned the famous and fabulous Paris hotel that bears its name, you did me a fairy-tale kindness that banked for me so much magic in my lifetime that I'm still drawing on it whenever I'm short of the currency of wonder.

When I was a college senior, in the fall of 1977, I was planning to meet my then-sweetheart in Paris over Christmas. He'd been in West Africa as a Peace Corps volunteer since the previous fall; we hadn't seen each other since then.

His birthday fell over Christmas week, and I wanted to do something special for it and to celebrate our reunion in your wonderful city, the city of Rick and Ilsa, Marius and Cosette, Swann and Odette. Mark and Pam?

One autumn day in Northampton, as I was (I swear this is the ridiculous truth) shaving my legs with gel and a disposable razor over that day's *New York Times,* out of sheer boredom I looked down at the story I was scraping myself over and idly began reading. It was an account of how you were redecorating the hotel, since it had passed to you after your husband's death. The article was interesting in itself, with its nod to Hemingway's drinking in the bar, but what captivated me about the story was your picture: that of a petite blonde lady with eyes so lively they shined through newsprint. Your hands were open as though you'd been caught in mid-explanation of some delightful anecdote from the hotel's most glittering days.

I looked into your black-and-white face, and dawn broke upon me.

And so it came about that, my legs a crazy map of razor-cleared paths, I hopped to my desk for a yellow legal pad and a BiC and sat down on the newspaper to draft you a letter. In it I explained about my reunion with my sweetheart and asked if, knowing how crowded Hemingway's bar and the hotel restaurant would be over Christmas week, I might secure a champagne or dinner reservation one night with which to surprise him.

Legwork hastily abandoned under the bathtub faucet, I copied the letter over on my Eaton's stationery in cartridge pen and mailed it off with a guesstimate of U.S. domestic stamps to MADAME RITZ, THE RITZ HOTEL, PARIS, FRANCE.

I have never believed since that heartfelt letters go unread or that dreams, in the end, go ignored.

You wrote me back by return mail that you would be delighted if, instead of a drink or dinner, I and my beau would be your guests overnight at Hôtel Ritz and that you "looked forward" to making our stay a comfortable and happy one.

Oh, Madame! Your dear, charming self gave me an experience and a memory that I treasure for eternity, from the moment we arrived by taxi and the concierge told us to wait, s'il vous plaît, then returned with you, who welcomed us so warmly with kisses on both cheeks. (My beau was dazed.) You had champagne chilling in a silver ice bucket with two crystal glasses at the ready in the aqua room that was ours, with its fabric-covered walls and marble fireplace. We were awed at the fresh, rosy tulips (How, at December's end?), blooming in a cut-crystal vase atop the mantel. The marble bathtub was so spacious we joked we could swim laps in it. The plush matching white terry robes with their generous sashes . . . the ivory down

feather comforter that so lightly kissed us with its
warmth . . . the next morning's *le petit dejeuner* cart set for
an early tea party, with its fresh violets, flaky croissants
hot in their white linen bed jacket, and strawberries red
and sweet as candy. . . . The feeling of pure happiness
that comes when you're again with your beloved after a
long separation, before you begin to remember, before you
begin to forget.

He, by the way, was glassy-eyed with culture shock by
the time breakfast arrived, but I felt like Eloise at the
Plaza.

I don't know the right words with which to thank you
for an experience and a memory like this. Sometimes now,
twenty-one years later, as many years as I was young then,
I find myself thinking about it, or retelling the story, and
then catch myself drawing in breath as I realize again, *This
really happened to me.*

I don't even know whether you're still alive to read this
letter—I so hope you are—but I must tell you how
grateful I am to you still for the gift you gave us of beauty
and comfort and luxury in that one night that has lasted
me a lifetime.

Because of course we were totally, utterly broke; him on
his Peace Corps stipend in the Third World, me a last-
semester college student on financial aid. We'd both
borrowed the money from family members to even *get* to
Paris when it became clear he couldn't go as far from
Africa as home. And we would be forced to accept a
stranger's help before our time together in your city was
over.

We left Hôtel Ritz on December 24 and took the metro
to a youth hostel Mark had found in a guidebook. That

night we went to midnight mass at Notre Dame, and a thousand voices swelled in holy praise and gratitude.

Having just met an angel, I was especially awed that Christmas Eve.

Merci, dear Madame, for both your gracious hospitality and its lifelong inspiration for me to go the extra kilometer when it comes to granting someone's wish. That's what makes the difference between a drink at a hotel bar and a night at the Ritz in Paris.

With love and gratitude always,

Mme. Pamela Janis

Dear unknown American woman in a cafe near the Rodin museum in Paris sometime during the first week of January 1978,

I never learned your name, hadn't even noticed you sitting there alone. But it seems you were at the next table, outside on that cold day, too, and overheard the grave conversation taking place at ours.

We'd been low on funds to begin with, had no credit cards to our name, had underestimated what Paris would cost on even the barest-bones budget during Christmas week, and then my wallet was stolen at Chatelet–Les Halles. So my boyfriend, Mark, and I were trying to figure out what to do next.

"Pardon me," you said, suddenly standing beside us. "I couldn't help hear. . . . I would like very much to give you this." You held out a 500-franc bill.

"No, we couldn't possibly . . ." we began, embarrassed, ashamed. "Thank you, but . . ."

"I insist," you said. "You need it, and I don't."

We were silenced by your honesty.

Finally I said, "How can we ever thank you?"

You answered, "By doing the same for someone else when you can."

And yes, thanks to you, I have, but I still want to say how very grateful we both were to you at that moment too.

Sincerely,

Pam Janis

Dear Aunt Stefanie,

Thank you for being the aunt with whom I share the most.

We both love books, scenery, Italy, Georgia O'Keeffe, animals, the Silver Palate and New York Times cookbooks and exploring the crevices of people's minds. To know the unique way in which someone thinks, what delights or depresses them, what makes them behave the ways they do——is there anything more fascinating?

As a reporter, I'm an amateur at this, but you're a professional. I confess I haven't always been comfortable with the fact that you're a psychologist; I used to think this meant you could read my (and everyone else's) mind. Not a happy prospect when you're still sorting things out and suspect you hate certain people and things about your life. (In other words, when I was a teenager.)

But you never pushed the psychology——you knew when and how to be just an aunt. ("Just an aunt!" Sorry, it "just" slipped out; I didn't mean anything by it.)

I remember how excited we all were when you received your Ph.D., and although I was too young to understand what a Ph.D. was, I knew it was something that made you special and a little different from other people, even my father, your brother. So did your apartment off Central Park West, and your divorce. I'd never known anyone before who had any of those things. To me you were like Beezus's Aunt Beatrice in Beverly Cleary's *Beezus and Ramona,* one of my favorite books. (So Aunt Beatrice was an elementary school teacher, drove a yellow convertible, and had never been married; Beezus had an unusual aunt, and so did I.)

The sense that you were special, that you were living a different and more surprising life than my parents and the people they knew (all married, with children, it seemed), was what first made me curious about *your* mind and feelings. I have to laugh now, because I realize that the subtext of all this was "Single" and *I* appear destined to be perceived as the same awe-evoking rarity by my niece Shoshi as you were by me. (You're laughing, aren't you? You were single, *plus* you could read people's minds. That makes you absolutely the first person who impressed me.)

Don't worry; it seemed just as cool to me later on when you got married, bought the house in White Plains and had Deborah. You even did that in a singular, pardon the expression, way: yours was the first "natural childbirth" labor I'd ever heard of, and my cousin was born on that most promising of days, January 1. (Beezus's Aunt Beatrice got married, too, in one of the later books.)

It wasn't until I was an adult, some years after my father died, that I felt I really got to know you. You moved from a background to a foreground presence after that (or does it just seem that way?). I don't recall exactly when we began to talk more and our talks became more open, but it does seem as though we were both waiting for the right time to know and relate to each other as adult women.

Since then, what a trove of surprises I've found in you, Aunt Stefanie! Thank you for your considerable insights about our family's history and dynamics. Thank you for sharing with me some of your professional writings on the subjects that engage your keen mind most fully. Through your analyses and inquiry on Emily Dickinson's poetry, dreams and death, I've learned how your intellect probes words, images and the ultimate sleep, reading meanings into meanings into meanings. Thanks to you, I first got curious about and then explored both Freud and Jung, and though I suspect you think I'm a total flake when it comes to spirituality, me with my amethyst crystal jewelry and Shirley MacLaine sensibilities, you nevertheless sent me the perfect birthday present one year: the book on Jungian interpretation of the tarot. How did you ever find it?

(Parenthetically, let me just add here that when I interviewed Shirley MacLaine in New York for a *Detroit News* story last year, the PR guy warned me away from asking her anything about spirituality. When I asked her—not him—why, she said, "Reporters turn it into a joke." If she'd only known to whom she was saying that! Okay, you can stop rolling your eyes now.)

The Jungian tarot book was so you because it was so me. (Is this transference or projection?) What I mean by that is that you're the rarest of gift givers: the thought that counts for you is the thought of the recipient. Thank you for always choosing the thing that surprises people not because it's so outrageous but because it's so right for them.

Here's the kind of personality marksman you are: Do you remember that for my Smith graduation twenty years ago you gave me Ralph Lauren perfume? Guess what—it's still my scent. Ralph Lauren gets my thanks, too, but you were the one who thought of it for me, specially. (Although in the early '80s so many women wore it that my fellow reporter at *The Daily Register,* Larry Haas, used to say it smelled like the Upper East Side. Regardless, it's me.)

You may think of yourself as cerebral, Aunt Stefanie,

but I'd have to say that your intuition is pretty tuned in too. I think for your next birthday, I'll give you an amethyst crystal and *Don't Fall Off the Mountain*.

Thank you for your brainy, conscientious, empathic, and sensitive aunthood. I'm sure you're a great psychologist, but I'm glad you're my aunt and not my therapist.

In this life.

Just kidding.

Love,

Pam

Dear Woody Allen,

It's not the first time you've heard from me, but I
wanted to say thanks again for the Moose and the
Berkowitzes routine, "The Whore of Mensa" (still my
absolute favorite Woody Allen short story—*"For one-fifty,
you could listen to FM radio with twins"*); *Play It Again, Sam;
Annie Hall;* and all the other ways you've made me laugh
over the years since my Smith friend Amy-Jill Levine first
began playing your stand-up routine LPs for me
sophomore year. (Thanks, Amy-Jill.)

Is there a baby boomer speechwriter in the country
who hasn't opened at least a couple of commencements
with these great lines from your "My Speech to the
Graduates":

> *More than any other time in history, mankind
> faces a crossroads. One path leads to despair and
> utter hopelessness. The other, to total extinction.
> Let us pray we have the wisdom to choose correctly.*

You gave the *yeedin* and the *goyim* a common language:
at a recent baby shower, a bunch of both of us sat around
laughing at The Scene in *Everything You've Always Wanted
To Know* . . . *"Go back! Go back!"* (You can guess the
context.) Once on-line, my friends Brooks Clark and Gary
Belis and I held a three-way script war that began with
this cc-ed e-mail: *"The moose mingles. Did very well."*

I wonder how many there were of us in the '70s and
'80s who headed for Woody Allen's New York. Now
twenty-somethings are going to the *Friends'* and *Seinfeld*'s
New York—do they realize Jerry Seinfeld went to yours?

I certainly did, and I want to thank you for it. For that and a letter you wrote to me in 1979 that I've saved forever.

During my first year in New York, I once went to Michael's Pub on a Monday night to hear you play clarinet and see you in person. I got on the line there with all your other fans between sets and introduced myself to you. There was so much I wanted to ask you and tell you and thank you for, but you asked about *me* instead; where I'd grown up, gone to school, what my parents did, what my life's plans were.

To be a writer, I told you. Like you. The conversation ended; it was time for the next set. But I wrote you pages and pages more the next day and mailed it, thinking, Well, at least I can say I've met Woody Allen.

Two days later, by return mail, BiC blue on Eaton's brown stationery, came a lovely thank-you to *me* from *you*, with this long-cherished message:

". . . I hope all goes well in your quest to write . . ."
You signed it, *"W.A."*
Thanks, W.A., for your art and letter.

Sincerely,

Pam Janis

Dear Brooks and Gary B.,

Thanks for being my Rob and Buddy, who are, in fact, buddies themselves. One of the great things in life, I think, is when friends you know from different times and places who have been hearing you talk about each other for years finally meet and hit it off.

You're both such kindred spirits that I have to stretch my memory to recall our first meetings—it seems like you've always been in my life. There are friends in life you date. . . . I *mean* date to a specific time or experience; the summer you got your driver's license, that time the office was being remodeled and you had to share a cubicle for nine weeks. Not you guys, though.

Thanks for being two friends I could never date.

        Love,

        Sally

Dear Uncle Arthur,

I hope you don't think this is silly, because I have
many, many things to thank you for in my life, but I'll
start with Chinese food.

All my life, it seems, I've loved it.

My parents were always crazy for it—even though my
mother was kosher about everything else. Caroline, Michele
and Gordon also love it; always have. Michele married a
rabbi's son and had the rehearsal dinner at a Chinese
restaurant—hold the pork. When I went to Paris last year
to visit Caroline and Malcolm, my first meal there wasn't
French; it was Chinese. I spent so much time wandering
around San Francisco's Chinatown two summers ago,
trying to decide whether to take that job in Seattle, that
the woman at the Kowloon Vegetarian Restaurant, on
Grant Street, had the tongs in the sticky bun tray when
she saw me on the threshold. (As it turned out, I didn't
get the job, but I did get a world-class American Express
bill from all the West Coast Chinese restaurants I ate dim
sum in thinking about it.)

So, you're probably wondering, what does any of this
have to do with you? You and Aunt Harriet have always
been kosher.

Well, there must have been at least one kosher Chinese
restaurant in Chinatown, because my mother remembers
going for a memorable meal there with you and Aunt
Harriet when she was sixteen and you two were dating.

It wasn't her first time eating Chinese, but something
about that meal was so good—or maybe it was the
memory of doing something special with her older sister
and her sister's boyfriend—that made the story stick in my

mind as the foreshadowing of her kids' love of the stuff. Then, of course, she met my dad, who'd spent fifteen months in Asia during the Korean War, so between the two of them it must have been meant to be that we'd all vote, hands down, for Chinese when they took us to restaurants. In fact, my mom says, each of our first restaurant meals, before we were all two, was Chinese.

It's so odd that I've never shared a kosher Chinese meal with you—certainly not the other kind, which my mother explained long ago went against the Orthodox way of life. Yet you have nieces and a nephew who would kill for a Full Kee soy half chicken. And I think of you and that treasured meal of my then-teenaged mother's whenever I pick up chopsticks.

Go figure.

I think this business with the Chinese food is actually a lot like some of the other ways you've been in our lives: a quiet but definite—and defining—presence.

When my dad died so suddenly, you were the one who told me how serious the long-term prognosis had been and how his not having to endure almost certain suffering was really a blessing for him. I hadn't thought of it that way. You made things kind of make sense.

It's just easier to thank someone for something like your love of Chinese food than for the years of love and guidance he gave as he watched you—and helped you—grow up.

Love,

Pamela

Dear IBM,

My dad worked for you while I was growing up; he was one of the editors of *THINK* magazine. After he died, in 1976, you hired my mother, first in a job at a spin-off company, then eventually as a *THINK* researcher.

I never thought about what my dad's job at IBM meant while I was growing up, except to notice that your 1960s dress code meant that every time he asked me to run upstairs and fetch something from the pocket of his "dark suit," I had to go through every suit he owned. I don't think many of the ties we gave him on Father's Day made it into the office, either. Some kids of high-tech company parents today never see their dads in shirts and ties; I never saw mine in a polo shirt. Come to think of it, I never saw him in a blue, yellow, or pink oxford, either.

Off my dad would go each morning to White Plains in his white plains. I've grown fond of that mental picture over the years, just as I grew fond of the company-leased Selectric typewriter in his study.

I know a lot of people probably write to thank you today for your computers.

To be honest with you, I have a Mac.

What I'm writing to thank you for instead is employing both my parents, the one who first supported our family and then the one who continued the job.

Thank you very much for making it possible for them to do this.

Sincerely,

Howard Janis's daughter, Pam

Dear Professor Ken Goldstein,

I don't think I've enjoyed a class more than your RW1
(Reporting-Writing One) section at Columbia's journalism
school in the fall of 1979, back in the Jurassic Age when
the dozen or so would-be scribes assigned to you were
banging out copy on deadline on the school's manual
typewriters.

With me you began at the top of the inverted
pyramid—I had trouble with news leads. After years of
hearing family tales from my mother that began with
"Now, this is a story altogether"—despite Daddy's J-school
Class of 1951 influence—you had to constantly remind me
to lead with active verbs, put in the number killed or
injured and break down the vote unless it was unanimous,
in which case say so.

With your adjunct professor, *New York Times* reporter
James Feron, you somehow managed to get it into my
wordy head that brevity was the soul of daily journalism.
But I never was a hard news talent and so am all the more
grateful that one of your great gifts as a teacher was
identifying—and championing—your students' individual
voices.

The stories you had our class running around the city
covering that semester were a New York history lesson in
themselves: a day at Mayor Ed Koch's City Hall; the pope's
visit to the U.N.; the Metropolitan Opera strike (there was
a Con Ed strike, a transit strike and a garbage strike that
year, too; it was like living in Italy); the Dalai Lama's visit
to the city; and a mob trial.

When I look back on that wonderful year, I think of
your warmth, enthusiasm and energy in and out of class

and realize that I came out of there with something more than basic journalism skills: you conveyed to me your passion for practicing both the art and the craft.

That's why I feel grateful and privileged to have a byline. And to have gotten to know you and your dear Irene.

I came to Columbia with two things, Ken: a love of the written word and an ambition to be a reporter. Thank you for turning those into decent copy.

. . . Uh-oh, I think I might have buried the lead.

By Pamela R. Janis

Dear Jeff Lynne,

Yours is a name I know only from record and
CD labels, but I've known it for a long time, ever
since I first heard the Electric Light Orchestra in my
friend Kim Cunningham's room freshman year at
Smith. I think the first album I heard of yours was
A New World Record, but I've listened to them all
so many times since then that I really can't
remember.

I wanted to let you know how much I've enjoyed my
ELO collection, CDs for at home, cassettes for traveling. I
especially love the strings section.

Your music sounds as creative and original to me today
as it did two decades ago. I can't analyze it—I don't know
enough about music to know why it sounds so good—but
I continue to appreciate it.

A lot of music heard years later brings back instant
memories of a single time, place and experience. It's
not that way for me with yours; "Telephone Line" or
"Evil Woman" is just as likely to evoke memories for me
of a car ride to Dulles Airport in 1996, a Halloween
party in 1985, or an afternoon in Kim's room in
1974.

ELO is never "background" music for me; even when I
try to do other things, your orchestration so completely
engages me that I forget to pay attention to whatever else I
thought I'd try to get done. I gave up trying to pay bills to
"Can't Get It Out of My Head" a bunch of years, and
crossed-out and initialed checks ago, because I really
couldn't.

Thank you for producing this great classical and classic rock that I've enjoyed so much.

Sincerely,

Pam Janis

*"Oh-Oh come take my hand,
We're riding out tonight to case
the promised land. . . ."*
—BRUCE SPRINGSTEEN

To Vicki Barker

I

For the sonnet you wrote back on 4 Aug.
in '78 or '79
To one whose first love was Deputy Dawg,
Thanks for penning those syllables and lines.
Your first love being Huckleberry Hound,
Ours must be the friendship of the ages.
We met in Kenyon's muddy April bounds;
Since then, a history writ in pages.
Through school, then roommates twice (New York, D.C.),
Thank you for both beyond-riotous stints.
Starred twins like Gemini (Laverne, Shirley?),
But always you in broadcast, me in print.
We're sure we were sisters in a past life,
But, zounds, could one have been the other's wife?

II

For all the nights we played games: Scrabble, gin.
You're best at Trivial Pursuit and GHOST.
I'd call it a draw in Concentration.
Thanks for not gloating though you won the most.
Our music: Bruce Springsteen, Southside Johnny,
Suite for Piano and Flute—Jean Rampal.
Thanks for forbearing my ferret, Connie,
Us three, the lone straights in Dupont Circle.
Could anyone's twenties be as much fun

as mine was with you, friend most enduring?
Your stellar career took you to London.
Thanks for the phone bills you've been incurring.
I call you first, both to giggle and wail.
What would we do without voice and e-mail?

III

Thank you for bridging time zones and war zones,
For sharing cramps to sushi, herbal tea.
Cuba, Turkey, Iraq: for finding phones.
As long as I've known you, I still worry.
It makes me cry that we still laugh like loons;
to think about the years we've been best friends.
If we measure our lives in news org spoons,
we count Gannett, NBC, CNN.
Oh, sorry, I left out the BBC.
But I've never heard your show, so instead
Thank you for your tour of the Tuileries;
We shrieked our way through rain and mud, feet lead.
It's true that we will always have Paris,
But why is it fate never does spare us?

IV

Vicki, so many things to thank you for.
My life wouldn't be as rich as it is
if our young nights hadn't been so sleep poor.
When ev'ry date meant an "I'm home" pop quiz.
When the word "BATS!" would convulse us in mirth.
(It still does, as do "weasel" and "guano.")
When a true poet knew a good word's worth.

Way too much Scrabble: why I got mono.
Thank you for your insights, intuition,
your loyalty and wit that have no end.
Wherever you are, my dear Great Woman,
Thank you for being my always-there friend.
For all the thank-yous that aren't here heard,
I hope that you can read between the words.

Dear Caroline,

I have such an eclectic collection of things to thank you for, which may be true for all sisters, but it seems to be especially true from me to you.

My thanks to you range from great underwear (I'll explain) to always remembering to send birthday cards early enough from Europe to get here on people's actual birthdays, and postcards from wherever you, Malcolm and my love of a nephew, Gregory, vacation. There's also your generous hospitality, first in London and now in Paris, to assorted family members who show up and get sick immediately upon arrival (ahem, yes, I am still embarrassed about that), and then have the chutzpah to invite their friends who are also overseas to your American Thanksgivings. (And it was a Thanskgiving to do Mom proud too. She knows, because she was there.)

It's funny; even though we were kids together, I have a much clearer sense of you as the woman you grew up to be. When I think of what I'm grateful to you for and why I admire you, much of it comes from the brave way you've tackled an adult life filled with challenges no one else in our family has experienced. I was the one who did everything first as a kid—because I was the oldest—but you are the one who's done everything first as an adult. You were the first to get married, first to buy a house, first to have a baby, first—maybe forever the only—to live outside the States.

When I've told you how brave I think you are to "bloom where you're planted," as the name of one of your Paris support groups puts it, you say, "No, I'm not—I didn't have a choice!" To me that makes you even braver—because when you made Malcolm your choice, you were choosing to take whatever came with a life far from home. (I'll continue to argue the case with you till *les vaches* come home, too.)

So I thank you for the lessons of a courageous life. Whenever I'm daunted by a new situation, I think of how resourceful you are and figure I can handle whatever too. I thought about this a lot when I was considering moving to Seattle to work for Boeing—it would have been a *huge* change for about 777 reasons—and I just wasn't sure *I'd* bloom where I was planted. (Not that I wouldn't have been watered enough there.) So, naturally, by the time I heard that I didn't get the job, your determined *c'est la vie* attitude toward getting over small and big fears had convinced me I'd be fine there.

No question about it, you're the one of Howard and Lucille's four kids who got the most highly developed aesthetic genes. Thank you for your good taste in everything from china and glassware to clothes and note cards; I hope your eye for the exquisite has given me more of one.

Your penchant for fine china especially has given me great hopes in the romance department—I bet there's no one else in the world who met her husband on a train to London from the Wedgwood factory in Stoke-on-Trent. The fact that the factory was closed that day for a bank holiday is beside the point. I'll always be grateful to you for showing me (and a bunch of other amazed people who know the story, most of whom came to Virginia from two continents for the wedding) that when one allows the winds of fate to carry them, one is *always* in the right place at the right time.

All right, the underwear: believe it or not, this ties in with your wedding.

Do you remember that day when you, Michele and I were all getting dressed in your hotel room? How you guys started teasing me because my underwear was so . . . uninspired? I'd never thought about undergarments as a fashion statement before, let alone a statement of self-expression. You and Michele were wearing great lingerie—and not just because it was your wedding day; you told me you wore good stuff *every* day. The two of you were merciless when we started to get bare naked, as we used to call it, and you saw the rips and runs of my white cotton rags. I believe the hateful phrase "Carter's Spanky Pants" was bandied about. Since Mom was too superstitious to have an "In case you're ever in an accident" underwear mentality, my foundation garb had never been attended to properly. This now seems amazing to me, considering I went to a women's college, but the fact is, before my two younger sisters reamed me out for looking like an undercover defective, I had never set foot in Victoria's Secret.

Well, never again did I appear in private underdressed. Thanks to you, I've now spent a small fortune on bikinis, briefs, bras, chemises, slips . . . You name it, I wear it. (Once when I was packing for a trip, my friend Ann Grimes looked into my open top drawer and announced, "You're sick.")

Thank you for dressing me down to undress myself up.

There is one thing from childhood I've been meaning to thank you for: your coinage of the term "munchkie." The whole family has used it to describe anything diminutive ever since you came up with it after first seeing the Munchkins in *The Wizard of Oz*. Munchkie. What a great adjective. Is there any other way to describe petits fours besides "munchkie"? Talk about a fully integrated life.

I'm writing you this letter about a month before Passover 1998, the first seder Greggy will share with his American grandparents, aunts, uncles and cousin Shoshi. It's strange to think that my nephew is learning to speak English and French at the same time, has one American parent and one British parent and will probably forever think of *us* as his foreign relatives. Yet there's something wonderful about a life that bridges nationalities, cultures, religions, languages, generations; all the borders people use to separate themselves from others. I think of you as raising a new international citizen who, thanks to his Mom/Mum/Maman, will always know how to bloom where he's planted.

As much as I miss you sometimes, I'm glad this life's experience chose you and that you're having it, despite its challenges, in all its richness. Thank you for sharing it so generously with me. I think of you whenever I play my Three Tenors CD, because it was in your living room that I first heard it, when you and Malcolm still lived in London. And also because it makes me think of the Three (Janis) Sisters, whose lives are as different, but as entwined, as those three magnificent voices.

Thank you for being such a loyal sister despite geography, different life's experiences and sometimes different points of view. But none of that matters, because when you strip our sisterhood to its bare nakedness, as we discovered folding laundry the last time I was in Paris, not only do we have the same genes; we have the same panties.

Love,

p_{am}

Dear Art Kamin,

Thank you for hiring me in my first reporting job at the *Daily Register*, "Monmouth County's Great Home Newspaper," as the slogan went.

I'll never know how you did it, but somehow you assembled a gang of twenty-something personalities and ambitions in a way that actually makes me look back fondly on zoning board meetings. (Not so much that I ever want to attend another one in my life, though.)

I had more fun with my fellow scribes in New Jersey than I ever would have believed possible for someone assigned to cover the Bayshore Regional Sewerage Authority. I think I may even still have a few black-Flair-on-white-AZK-notepaper memos from my *Register* days.

"Good job," you'd write when you liked a story. *"Many thanx."*

Being a *Reg* reporter *was* a good job, Art.
Many thanx.

Sincerely,

Pam Janis

Dear Beveridge and Garrison families,

I hardly know how to start, afraid that this letter will bring back sad memories.

Not knowing what's happened in your lives in the seventeen years since our paths crossed, I am hoping that the years have been good to you. I have often thought of you over the years as I continued with, then left, then resumed journalism. My prayers have always been with you.

I'm writing now because you played a part in the reason I left journalism, and also in why I came back, and I wanted to thank you.

Let me explain:

I was a twenty-four-year-old reporter, less than a year out of journalism school, at my first newspaper job in New Jersey. I was the reporter on Sunday duty at the *Register* the day after Sharon and Calvin died.

Sharon was just a year younger than me, Calvin only three years older.

When I recently reread the April 24, 1981, news story I wrote about the accident, I was reminded that Calvin was in a General Electric training program at the time. I spent a year at G.E. in the mid-'80s, and now I wonder at all the other ways our lives could have and might have crossed over the years. Perhaps we would have had absolutely nothing else in common, but at the time our ages seemed common enough ground.

It was my job to go after the story—tracking you down that day to get "comment."

I've never hated doing a story more in my life. What I really felt like doing was tracking down the drunk driver's parents and asking *them* for comment. But journalistic reality meant I had to find you. My editor smelled a "great story." And it was a "slow news day," so that meant it was "a page one."

At the time, the language we use as newsroom shorthand horrified me; two families had lost their children. I was embarrassed discussing how to "play" the story in chat with my editors, but that was nothing compared to actually making the phone call to you. Because, of course, we "needed" a picture of the engaged couple, whom you were already planning to bury in side-by-side graves.

To my eternal surprise, Mr. Beveridge, Sharon's dad, kindly invited me to come right over and even gave me directions.

When I got to the Beveridges' house on Irwin Place, embarrassed, timid, nervous about intruding on your most private hours, ready to receive the photo at the door and head for the hills—worried, even, that Mr. Beveridge had invited me over to yell at me about the invasive, intrusive, sensational, insensitive, goddamned media—something happened that has colored my life ever since.

He invited me inside to meet Sharon and Calvin's families.

My face flaming, I met you all, from Sharon's grandmothers down to a small child who I think one of you said was to have been the flower girl. I looked in your faces for resentment, but all I saw were welcoming nods.

"Sharon and Calvin were killed in a car wreck yesterday morning," Mr. Beveridge said. "That was only one day in their lives. We don't want them remembered for one sad day—we want people to know they lived happy lives."

So we talked, and you told me about those lives. About Calvin's being an electrical engineer. About Sharon's good business sense. About their shared Methodist faith and service to St. John's Church. About how they'd met at a church-sponsored swim party three years before and had been inseparable ever since. About the wedding that was to have been that September. And about the double funeral they would have wanted.

Here, Mr. Beveridge said, use this picture: see how happy they . . . were.

I went back to the newsroom and wrote my page one:

> *A young couple who planned to be married . . . police say . . . driver charged with running a stop sign, drunk driving and two counts of death by auto . . . families praised the South Aberdeen and borough first-aid squads, patrolmen and hospital personnel who assisted them yesterday.*

I remember you made a point of requesting that I put that last part in the story and how touched I was that, in the midst of your grief, your families wanted to thank the rescue squads in the newspaper.

I'm writing you this letter not to make you relive that awful day but to thank you for the many things I learned from your families then and have spent many years thinking about since.

It's true that I left journalism in 1983 and was gone for almost a dozen years, in part because I got what editors would call "emotionally involved" with the people I wrote about and their stories. Also because I was appalled by what I thought of as the "stick-a-mike-in-their-face-and-ask how-it-feels-to-lose-their-kid" brand of journalism. Clearly I couldn't work for editors I thought of as "heartless"; job, shmob.

More significant to me than my leaving journalism, though, is my return.

One thing your families impressed upon me that day— not only by sharing your children's stories with me but by imploring me to remember they were stories of two lifetimes, not just one day—is that journalism is a service profession. A story that has real weight and meaning has many more facts than simply what can be typed in a police accident report, heard in an eyewitness account or even seen in a snapshot of a smiling couple.

To tell someone's story is a responsibility to them and their loved ones, and also to the larger community. Before that day with you, I think I only had it half-down: to get the facts accurately. "Getting to the heart" of a story for me then meant getting to the *point*.

Now it means learning about the real hearts involved.

Some are closed to me, of course, but I always try to make the effort. I try to take care with hearts, because as a journalist, I am in service to them and to the people who will come to know something of them through my words.

So I thank you for showing me what I didn't learn at journalism school—that sources don't "give" you a story; they entrust you with one.

I can't write to all my sources, but if I could, I'd thank them all for sharing—for entrusting—their stories and secrets with me. They include a teenager battling anorexia, a woman whose famous father sexually abused her, a politician who lost his daughter to alcoholism, a woman who was once at the center of an international scandal, and many, many others.

And especially the Beveridges and Garrisons.

I am more indebted to you than I can ever express for inviting me into your home and your hearts the day I really became a journalist.

Thank you.

Sincerely,

Pam Janis

Dear Carol and Andy Davison and Gilbert Okun,

You three are not acquainted, but you have something in common: my gratitude for providing me, at different times in different places, with homes.

Carol and Andy, you rented me my first apartment as a lone dweller, sans roommate, in the basement of your wonderful second home, on Abbott Avenue in Ocean Grove, New Jersey, when I came to Monmouth County as a *Register* reporter in 1980. As a matter of fact, I found it in the *Register's* classifieds, sitting in the Shrewsbury Diner after the meeting in which the paper's editor, Art Kamin, hired me. My goal that day was to find a place *fast*. I never dreamed the first one I circled would lead me to you, as close to the boardwalk, beach and ocean as a house could be.

I loved that little basement apartment, with its two trundle beds, stall shower, door to the furnace room, and sea song. Thank you so much for renting it to me—and taking Connie, the ferret, along with her mom. I have never forgotten your kindness and warmth.

Gilbert, you rented to Connie too! This apartment, which I love so much I'm still in it twelve years later, became her geriatric home, but you let two more ferrets and a cat follow her. I was so afraid I wouldn't be able to find a place that allowed animals, but you said you were game for my game.

This cozy "1 BR w fireplace," as the *Washington Post* ad put it, has been the scene of one dishwasher replacement, two full-time jobs, three animals, four downstairs neighbors, five relatively major romances, and six years of freelance writing. I'd so hoped to get this apartment when you first showed it to me and was thrilled when you called with this news: "Miss Janis, your credit history checked out just fine." I loved it when I ran into you on weekends, usually when you were showing an apartment, and you'd call "Miss Janis!" just as I caught your eye. And I miss you now that you've retired and your able son Larry has stepped in.

I've been so fortunate to have had great friendships and great places to live. I'm grateful to you, as landlords, for providing both.

Thank you. Now I have to go write Larry a check for May.

Sincerely,

Pam

Toots, Toots, Toots!

Here I am in Calistoga—without you, which seems odd—knowing that thanking you for first bringing me to this beautiful, magical Napa Valley spa town is a lame way to begin a thank-you note to one of my dearest friends in the world, not to mention a truly Great Woman. Calistoga: our special place, a place I probably wouldn't have ever discovered if you hadn't brought me up here after you'd moved to San Francisco in '82, a move that left me, to use your word, "bereft," although two years at *The Daily Register* was enough for us both. I guess I'd always known you'd go home to the West Coast eventually. But in the sixteen years since you did, I've never stopped wishing we lived in the same place the way we did as reporters in New Jersey at the dawn of the Greed Decade. Which was goofier, do you think, that newsroom or that decade? I think the apocryphal moment of both came when the newsroom clock stopped on election night at the precise minute the networks called it for Reagan.

Thank goodness we were there long enough to form a lifetime sisterhood. Long enough to be forever Toots and Toots, the way Woody Allen and Tony Roberts called each other "Max" in *Annie Hall.*

I guess we should thank that sexist reporter for calling every waitress in New Jersey "Toots." If we hadn't been so indignant about that, he might not have started calling us Toots, too, and we might have stayed Kathy and Pam forever. I can't imagine such a thing.

Thank you for all the counsel, consolation, confidences, stories, secrets, listening, laughter, wit and wisdom—in a word, friendship—you've packed into all the years, Toots.

Considering that our first conversation was probably about a planning board meeting, it's nothing short of amazing that we've grown into our forties sharing everything that's been interesting, moving, surprising and hilarious about our lives. With some friends you share one experience—a senior seminar, a job, a group house, motherhood—and it's the nostalgia that lasts a lifetime, or less. With others, the Tootses, that experience is only the starting point of a friendship that grows in richness and intimacy as the years unfold. You, Toots, are a friend for all seasons and ages.

You're the friend who absolutely debunked for me that old saw *"Things change when friends get married and have children."* The only thing that's changed between us since David, Matthew and Halle made the scene is that I have three more friends and a second home in San Francisco. When I think about my most memorable times in life, many of them happened around your bleached-wood kitchen table. We've reached so many crossroads there: what to name Matthew; whether I should marry that guy; how to choose between our jobs and our passions; whether to order Indian, Italian or Chinese from Waiters on Wheels. I guess these are the sorts of conversations everyone has in life, but having them with you makes every one seem like an event to me.

One thing I definitely want to thank you for is marrying a doctor. One of us had to, to treat my perpetual travel malaises. Do you remember the day David and I met? I was in the city on a business trip, staying at the Union Square Hilton. This was back in the days of my Draconian cramps. I was in bed in the hotel with them, bummed out at being too incapacitated to meet the doctor/photographer who by then I was sure would be Dr. Toots.

David wanted to come over anyway; he evidently didn't think that a distended abdomen, heating pad and moaning like an accident victim should stand in the way of the introductions. He's the only friend I've ever met who said hello and then started doing acupressure on me. Thanks, David. And thanks for all the eye, ear and throat peerings, on-site prescriptions, and even long-distance diagnoses since.

This is one way you and I are different, Toots: you sail through bacteria zones that would level me—India, the Sudan, Halle's preschool—feeling fine. The difference between you and me is, you go to Mexico and see the ruins; I go to Mexico and *am* the ruins. But we do share one travel ruination, motion sickness. You even outclass me in this department: I never got sick on a ferry while it was docked. (Okay, okay, you were pregnant.)

Remember the time we took Matthew for a picnic lunch on Angel Island (a kid after my own heart—he wanted to see the angels)? You told me that morning that the Bay ferry ride was so brief and calm that even you didn't bother taking Dramamine. Four minutes into it, we were both as green as old glass Coke bottles. We seriously debated getting off at Tiburon, but we knew we'd never sell Matthew on the idea.

It didn't occur to either one of us to swap Tiburon's and Angel Island's names for a day and thus get off the damn boat sooner, because we'd never stretch a tale for the kids (except for the time when you told Matthew his missing Pooh bear had stayed in Michigan a few extra days to visit friends. Who, the Berenstains? At least that gave us time to procure a stand-in. Oh, my God, if he reads this letter when he's thirty, he'll know what we did).

So there we were aship, you sipping Coke at the prow and me trying to recall all the states in alphabetical order—I never know what to do with Washington, D.C., which gives me something in common with Congress.

Fortunately, the two Tootses made it to Angel Island with both lunch and breakfast intact (and immediately purchased Dramamine at premimum prices for the return trip). Matthew opened his little backpack full of dinosaurs, and never were Pooh, Piglet and Tigger as happy as we were munching salami and cheese on crusty bread and drinking cool water on that gorgeous bay day, visiting with angels.

That was the quintessential Toots caper: what would have been a normal recreational outing for most people capsized our cool and sank our cover as grown-ups. Some of life's journeyers come back with souvenirs; we always come back with stories just by being together, two women who still love Lucy with the fervor of Deadheads.

How many meals, picnic and otherwise, do you think we've shared since our Shrewsbury Diner days after work, anywhere from 2 to 6 A.M.? (The *Reg* reporters stopped going there at normal meal hours after one especially lively and graphic dinner discussion of the county's all-time greatest murders—typical reporters' talk—and a wan patron turned around in his booth and said, "Do you mind? People are *eating*." We fell momentarily silent, confused: now, what were we saying?)

We've shared a zillion meals and a zillion car trips on both coasts. Weekends in New Jersey, we'd head for New York in my car, the '72 Plymouth Duster, which Larry Haas named Vietnam II because it was a disaster that just kept on going. In the car, we caught up on the early years of each other's lives. I told you about my father's Home Barber Kit haircuts; you told me about your job as a Universal Studios tour guide the summer Lucille Ball got mad at the guides and you all sent her roses to make up.

I still can't believe there are parts of each other's lives we weren't there for. Now, on the ride from San Francisco to Calistoga, we fill in the details of the headlines we broadcast first by phone.

Thanks for always being such great company, Toots.

The one thing I regret in our long friendship is that I didn't meet your mother when she came to New York before she died. I would have liked to have known her, if only long enough to thank her for the daughter whose friendship I treasure. It's only now that we've gotten to the ages our mothers were when we left home that I realize how important it is to say and do things before it's too late and that we never know when that will be. I'm trying now to make thank-yous more like spot news than long-range reporting.

So, Toots, thank you for all of the above and also for reading and critiquing my writing through the years, from my Bayshore Regional Sewerage Authority meeting stories to the manuscripts of my various longer works. Thanks for wearing that silly raccoon face hat, twin to mine, that time we went to New England to see the fall foliage. Thanks for setting the agenda for our first, but by no means last, Great Women's confab in San Francisco ("Wednesday, 7 P.M.: Seminar on Legal Ramifications of Marrying Your Best Friend"). Thanks for making me one of the *chuppa* holders at your wedding. Thanks for loving the book of books on friendship itself,

Charlotte's Web, as much as I do. These sentences in it were written about you, Toots:

> " . . . *She was in a class by herself. It is not often that someone comes along who is a true friend and a good writer. . . .*"

And thank you too, Toots, for making peaceful Calistoga forever "our" place.

> Love always,
>
> *Toots*

Dear Jeff,

Okay, so we've talked maybe twice a year since we've been on opposite coasts post–journalism school; at last report we were both still single. Not that I want you to live an eligible bachelor's life forever or anything, but I do hope our deal is still on. I'm getting nervous as the big night gets closer.

Since it's now less than two years away, I just want to remind you that we agreed if neither of us was married by then, we'd celebrate it together.

And since things certainly seem to be moving in that direction, I just wanted to thank you in advance for promising that I'd have a New Year's Eve date for the millennium.

Love,

Your first date in the year 2000

TO: JERRY LUCAS, PRESIDENT AND CEO OF TELESTRATEGIES, INC.,
MCLEAN, VIRGINIA

Dear Jerry,

You are the only boss I've ever told he was nuts for
wanting to hire me, but this is a thank-you note for
corralling me anyway into one of the best, if most unlikely,
jobs I've ever had.

When you first asked me to come edit an industry
newsletter for your then start-up telecommunications
consulting firm, after those two weeks I temped for you in
1982—it was Christmas, I was broke, and I had yet to
find a reporting job in Washington—I admit it, I thought
you were out of your mind. I remember saying to you,
"Why do you want to hire someone for a
telecommunications job who doesn't even have cable?"
(Guess what: I still don't.)

"You're a reporter," you said. "You'll pick it up." You
had a twinkle in your eyes and an unmatched zeal for all
the exciting business opportunities that telephone
technologies suddenly promised in the brand-new wake of
the AT&T divestiture.

Your business seemed pretty dull to me, but then, I was
twenty-six and thought nothing but *The Washington Post*
would do. However, the *Post* wasn't exactly killing its
legendary post-Watergate self to hire me, and you seemed
sure this was a good idea. I thought, What the hell, if I
don't like it, I can leave.

It's always the places you plan on just running in for a
minute that you end up staying an hour. Or, in my case,
two-and-a-half years.

You did, in fact, give me enough of a telecommunications education to make me feel both competent and confident in my job. I am eternally grateful to you for teaching me a field that's been a surprisingly durable and portable employment resource for me. If anyone had told me in 1982 that I'd still be writing telecom speeches fifteen years later—and know what I was talking about—I frankly wouldn't have believed it. I never thought of myself as a businessperson until you made me feel I could do it with the same set of genes I could write and tell stories with. It doesn't matter that I eventually traded back business for journalism—your enthusiasm and the sheer fun of working for you gave me a great life's experience. Not to mention a lifetime friend in Martha Goodwin, my fellow "How did I land here?" newsletter editor.

When I think of the unbelievably narrow grooves we sometimes set ourselves in—and I was already thinking that way at twenty-six!—it makes me sad for what has to be a vast amount of lost creative potential in this world. Not to mention personal satisfaction. I had more fun in the job I thought would be a transition-time sleeper than I ever would have believed possible. I believe now that my life wouldn't feel half so colorful had I done *only* the thing I thought I could—and wanted—to do.

I'm also grateful to you for taking your young staff—do you know that we used to call ourselves "Jerry's Kids"?—everywhere to learn the business. New Orleans, San Francisco, Chicago, Miami, L.A. . . . I can't remember all the places we went, but you opened up more than the world of business for us; you opened up the country. And though you had almost twenty years on us, you seemed to have as much fun as we did.

Even if I live to outgrow my fixation with Mary Tyler Moore, I'll never forget that in Minneapolis, you had a cabbie take me past Mary Richards's house. Thanks for that fun surprise—and for coming along for the ride!

Thanks, too, for explaining why planes stay up.

One more thing: as I grew into the job you gave me and was asked to give speeches, I realized I could ace the writing but was scared to deliver them. The first time I had to give a speech, at a real estate conference in New York, you came with me. Midnight, the night before my breakfast debut, found us sitting in the Carnegie Deli. You said, "Okay, you're on."

"Good morning," I said, and we both fell out laughing. Then you said the magic words that saved me:

"Just remember," you said, "your audience is on your side. They're there because you know something they *want* to know. They've come to learn from you, and they *want* you to succeed in teaching them."

Oh, Jerry! You were as right on the money with public speaking as you were with so-called bypass telephone technologies. I've taken your words in the Carnegie Deli to heart again and again on behalf of my clients as I turn out those telecom (and other) speeches I thought I'd never know enough or care enough to write.

I feel unbelievably lucky that that temp agency first uplinked me to your barely unpacked company door. Thank you for all you've done to enlighten and enliven my professional life.

Sincerely,

Pam

Dear long-distance and local telephone companies,

Please don't take this letter to mean that I want to hear from any of you about "opportunities" to change my service provider; I'm deliriously happy with my long-distance company, okay? And just to make you crazy—as crazy as you make all women and men who hope that when their phones ring, it's someone other than you calling—I'm not going to mention which company I actually use. If you look me up in your records and I'm not there, it means that thanks to your annoying TV commercials, endless mail trying to sneak into my home in envelopes marked from airline frequent-flyer programs, and general marketing hype and overkill, I've already hung up on you.

Having said that, this is in fact a thank-you note.

I should probably be writing it to Alexander Graham Bell, but since he never personally put any of my calls through, I'm addressing it to you instead.

I've been grateful for the telephone ever since I was three and my mother had to leave me alone one afternoon when we still lived in Oceanside, New York. It seems inconceivable to me now that my mother would ever have left one of her kids alone for a nanosecond, so it must have been a dire five-minute emergency, but I have a very clear memory of her telling me two things as she left: 1) if I needed anything, all I had to do was pick up the receiver that she'd taken off the phone and placed on the table, and talk to Aunt Adele, who lived down the block and across the street; and 2) *Don't hang up the phone!*

Naturally, after she left, I had to test out this intriguing situation and began talking into the receiver. And Aunt

Adele talked back to me! Amazing! For months afterward, I didn't understand that my mother had first dialed Aunt Adele's phone number; I thought that the phone went only to Aunt Adele's house and that she would always be there to talk to whomever spoke into our receiver. Hearing a dial tone for the first time was a small personal heartbreak.

It seems so sweet now to think that there was a time in any neighborhood that a mom would feel the phone was protection enough from the world outside and another mom would have the time to commandeer her only line to keep an ear on a child.

Before call waiting, before speed dial and automatic redial, before area codes you can't identify, before answering machines, before beepers, before cellular phones, before annoying telemarketers who interrupt dinners and good moods, before all that, when every call was an important call, there was just the magic of talking to someone you couldn't see.

It's still magic to me, and that's why I'm writing this letter.

Thank you for connecting me over the years to everyone in my life at one time or another. The telephone has never ceased to seem miraculous to me. It's made it possible for me to always feel part of my far-flung friends' lives and make them part of mine. How lucky I feel to have best friends furlongs away from Washington, D.C., in places like Chicago, Dallas, San Francisco, London and Hawaii, with whom I never feel out of touch.

How grateful I am to be able to serve clients in places like New York, Montreal and Michigan, thanks to the phone.

I've met some of the most important people in my life

for the first time by phone: my Smith roommate, Mary Rumsey; my editor at the *Detroit News,* Alan Fisk; my friends Susan Hooper and Ann Grimes.

I've gotten great and terrible news by phone: my getting into graduate school; engagements; the births of my nephew and niece and friends' babies; a friend's cancer diagnosis; my father's death.

I've left ten-second messages and once talked to my friend Julie Pistone in Cleveland for four-and-a-half hours. We had to take bathroom breaks.

I'm writing this letter to thank all of you—local phone companies, too—because Americans, more than any of the world's other people, take for granted widely available, easy, clear, reasonably priced phone service, not to mention that lifesaver, 911.

The phone has instantly brought the people I love right next to me since the day Aunt Adele picked up.

Thank you for connecting me to her and to the thousands of dollars' worth of other people I've phoned or who have phoned me since.

But please don't call me anymore.

Sincerely,

Pam Janis

Dear Ann and Hoops,

I always think of you together because of the strange coincidence of knowing you both separately first. As much as my sister reporter at *The Register,* Susan, would talk about her best college friend, Ann, it never occurred to me that the Ann being discussed was my Kenyon friend Paul Grimes's sister. So now I'm convinced that God destined us all to meet one way or the other.

Ann, besides your friendship always, thank you for making or taking me to dinner so often when you were at the *Washington Post.* Having been a freelancer yourself, you, more than anyone just about, know the life's ups and downs, and it seemed you always called with just the right question at just the right time: "Are you doing anything tonight?" I'm especially grateful to you for taking charge when I was sick that time and couldn't swallow anything, it seemed, but your food. Thanks for your oven-roasted potatoes and also for your superb, first unofficial edits on my *Post* copy.

Oh, Hoops, you've been in Hawaii for more than ten years now, and I still miss you as much as I did when you first left Washington. Thank you for halting that dating whirl in my late twenties by telling me to "stay off the sauce." Thank you for coming up with that brilliant game with Vicki and Michele, Foreign Phrasebook, where we all make up typical guidebook English translations. (You started it off with "The letter is from Father. He is in Munich.") Thank you for all the giggles and AK47 conversations past and the ones that continue via phone, e-mail and your visits to the mainland.

Thank you for your lovely singing at Ann's wedding

and for singing with me on every possible occasion for which we can pen a parody.

Thanks, you two Great Women, for your words and music.

Love,

Pam

Dear Ben,

Thank you for proving the value of the yellow pages.

You weren't listed as a "Headhunter," which in 1985 I thought was a real term and so looked for it in the phone book, but when I finally found "Executive Search Consultants" and dialed your number because your ad in its box stood out, I found *you.*

"Send me your resume," you told me when I called. Frankly, I never thought anything would come of it.

Do you know that after your having placed both me and my sister Michele in jobs, and advising my brother, Gordon, we now affectionately refer to you as "the Family Headhunter"?

Michele and I also call you St. Ben.

Thank you for telling me, "For speechwriting, you *need* at least some corporate experience" and then sending me over to G.E. Information Services and my great year-long manager and colleague, Nancy Jamison (now McIlvain) and Steve Haracznak, respectively, to get it.

Thanks for keeping me in mind ever since. And for your always on-the-money counsel. Who else would have the answer to questions like "Is a tangerine-colored suit too much?" (Your answer: "Definitely don't wear it to the *first* meeting.")

Thanks, Ben, for finding me a job when I needed one, and for staying a friend.

Sincerely,

Pam J.

Dear Pops,

Thank you for marrying my mother.

No, wait, I didn't mean it like that!!! Not "Thank you for marrying her and taking her off our hands," but *"Thank you for marrying her and making her happy again."*

I really mean it.

The week my dad died in 1976 was the first week my mother had ever been a "me" instead of a "we." As she's told us often, she shared a room—even a bed—with her two sisters while she was growing up and even through NYU. She switched bed partners a week after graduation when she married my dad.

When he died two decades later, she felt as alone in the world as she did in her own room. Having four kids was beside the point. We really might as well have been chopped liver for all the adult company we could provide her.

I was the best she could do in that department for the two weeks I was home from college—because in one of those weird synchronicities of the world, my extremely education-minded father made sure I didn't miss any school by managing to have his *shiva* coincide with spring break.

My mother asked me to be her roommate while I was home, because she couldn't bear the nights alone. Suddenly a widow at forty-two, she was only a year older than I am now. Hard to believe, isn't it?

You'd think this would have been terribly maudlin, two stunned, lost-feeling women, one newly minus her husband, the other, her father, damply sharing a king-size bed. Two women, each of whom thought the other was impossible to be around on the *best* of days.

Believe it or not—don't even try to figure this out—we actually had some good times not being able to sleep through the worst nights of my mother's life. We talked. She told me then that her greatest fear was growing old alone.

"Oh, really?" I said. "What are you going to do when [my dad's only single friend, read: homely] asks you to marry him?" My mother almost fell out of bed laughing.

"Oh, my God, you're right," she said. "But who else is ever going to marry me?"

Almost immediately, she started crying, because she realized all over again she'd lost her soulmate. And she really was afraid: who else *was* ever going to marry her?

Is that the way you felt, too, when Marge died?

I know it took you a few years longer than you bargained for to marry Mom after you first met her at that newsman's memorial service in 1980—she loves it that John Chancellor made the introductions—but who would have figured she'd sell the house in Stamford and move to McLean, Virginia? Bet you didn't count on having a long-distance relationship in your sixties.

But that People's Express and Amtrak courtship was the most charming one ever. For the first time in my mother's life, she was going on overnight dates with a man who delighted in doing everything New York had to offer. She especially loved *Cats*. Every weekend, she came home with two things: a big smile and a loaf of rye bread. The best in New York, she said every Monday. We thought she meant the rye bread.

Mom was having such a good time keeping company

with you, as she called it, that she was dragging those size-9 heels a bit about getting married. If anyone had told me eight years earlier that that would be the case, I frankly wouldn't have believed it. But now there was this huge Thing in the road for her: how would her by-then-grown kids deal with a stepfather? And how would her childless beau deal with her four grown kids?

As we all know, she made up her mind one Saturday afternoon when her plane landed in Newark and you weren't waiting there for her, beaming, as usual.

In fact, you'd been knocked over by some huge Thing in the road on your way to Port Authority to catch the bus to the airport—was it a bicycle messenger? Taxi? Rye bread truck? Who knows; you were the victim of a hit-and-run.

When Mom heard the news—they paged her—she made up her mind in the People's Express waiting area to marry you. Please do me a favor: don't ever give any of my dates pointers on how to impress a woman.

You dealt with the grown-kids thing brilliantly by taking us to an all-you-can-eat hotel buffet brunch. Introductions over, we told you, Fine, she's yours. My only question was what to *call* you. We were ages twenty-one to twenty-nine at the time; our "Dad" days were done. "I can't exactly call you 'Pops,' " I said for laughs. "Sure you can," you said. So I did. I do.

Which is what you and my mother both said for the second time at your wedding in 1985. A great day for her, and us.

We're glad you made the move to McLean—but we miss the rye bread like hell.

Who wrote this script? My mother, a woman who loves to talk more than anything else in this world (except maybe her kids), marries a retired RADIO PRODUCER. Believe me, I couldn't make up anyone better for her than you. In more ways than one.

I should be so lucky to find a man who puts fresh flowers in the house every week, loves old movies and new books and plays gin like nobody's business.

A friend who recently became a stepmom says the "step" part comes not, as you'd think, from being a step away from the biological role but from quietly noting an absence and "stepping in."

Boy, with the four of us did you really step in it.

Thank you for making my mother so happy, first by marrying her and then by becoming our stepfather.

Love,

*D*am

Script: Davey—Final Draft

"Dave Leonard . . . My best friend without ovaries . . . My video partner of ten years . . . Sorcerer to my apprentice.

Matched up as Gannett corporate staffers on a blind creative date in 1987 to produce a video marking USA Today's fifth anniversary . . . We were both skeptical at first that this collaboration would work out.

I knew only words; you knew only pictures. . . . Some team. But this was an assignment, not a choice. . . . So we sat down to dream up a video. . . .

. . . And realized we were in big trouble. The task was huge; we had a gazillion Gannett locations to shoot in, and we basically had a month to do the job.

At which point you asked Gannett's dad for the keys to the company jet to speed up our travel itinerary— and got it.

I knew then I was in the presence of true greatness.

(Music Transition)

*. . . Sometime during that wild ten-day ride . . . In
Anaheim or Olympia, Louisville . . . or Kansas
City . . . St. Cloud, Minnesota, or Needham,
Massachusetts, where we shared the Holiday Inn with
a confab of vaccuum-cleaner salesmen . . . Iowa City
or Detroit . . .*

*. . . Somewhere along the way . . . You made me see
how the shots we were taking of presses and news
racks and people reading the paper in every city we
went to told a story . . . And how the words of the
USA Today-ers we shot fit the pictures.*

*. . . And our future as both creative partners and
friends was storyboarded.*

Thank you for helping me see what you saw . . .

. . . Pictures and possibilities . . .
. . . Montages and meanings . . .
. . . Scenes and segues . . .

*Who would have believed the visual and literal could
work together quite like that?*

*. . . Or that I'd remain so linear that, when I moved
offices, I'd have to call my conceptual partner to fold
the flat cardboard things Building Services brought
me . . . into boxes . . .*

. . . Or that I still need you to set my VCR?

But then who would have believed I'd be an usher at your wedding. Or that I'd come to make your Capitol Hill house my second home . . . Your wonderful wife, chef Marcia, my good friend . . . Or your son, Skyler, my special pal . . .

Who would have believed I'd spend so many nights with a man I wasn't dating?

. . . In edit suites and post houses . . . Pondering the ten- or fifteen-second dissolve . . . Laying down music tracks . . . Gulping Coca-Cola and coffee . . . Exhausted and eating crap for weeks on end.

But always having fun yet.

Thank you for teaching me everything you knew about production in those cold rooms, Davey.

Thank you for shlepping the equipment and luggage through every airport in the country, it seems. . . . Many of them at five in the morning, when as you unfailingly pointed out to me, I did not look my best, thank you.

On the last flight I caught with you as a Gannett employee . . . A flight from LaGuardia to Dulles we would have missed had it not been running late, you said, "I have something to ask you."

I looked at you, expecting you to say, "Did everyone we shot sign releases?" . . . But you unbuckled your seat belt and got down on one knee.

Thank you for proposing that I still be your creative partner even after I left Gannett.

(Music Transition)

While I was there . . . Thank you for helping make corporate culture livable for me by wearing your Mickey Mouse ears with your gold-stitched name when I wore mine in our brainstorming meetings and defending the explanation that they were our thinking caps.

Thank you for graciously agreeing that if a meeting ever were, in fact, to go on so long that I died in it, you would remove my pantyhose.

Thank you and Marcia both for being there in my time of carpal tunnel need. Thanks, Marcia, for making me so many great dinners. Thanks, Davey, for cutting them up for me.

Thank you for telling me that the way a video script works is that right about here the scriptwriter should "bring 'em home to Jesus."

When I said, "Put that in terms a Jewish woman can understand," you said, "Okay: bring 'em home to Bloomingdale's."

. . . Thank you, partner, for all the imagination and care you bring to the coproduction of a friendship whose running time can never be too long for me."

—END—

Dear Oreste Cafe in the Rosslyn section of Arlington, Virginia,

Thank you for the great sausage-and-pepper heroes you make.

Sincerely,

The woman who always gets the Utz Grandma's potato chips, too, and thinks halfway through the bag, "I really didn't need these."

Dear Joe,

You've made it impossible for me to ever move; I wouldn't trust anyone else with my car. Come to think of it, since you're at Chevy Chase Chevyland, you've also made it impossible for me to ever own anything but a GM car. You're not just a crack mechanic; you're vital to the U.S. economy.

Thank you for all your great work over my Chevette and Geo Prizm years. That doesn't even begin to cover the bits of our lives we've shared during scheduled maintenance visits (the red Prizm hatchback) and unscheduled repairs (the light blue Chevette). On your side, we'd catch up on the dating front before you were married and the family developments after. On my end . . . still nothing new. If anything breaks between oil changes, I'll let you know.

I was referring to news of my marital status, not my transmission.

My notes on the overnight-slot envelope have now begun "Attn: Joe Lyons . . ." for . . . can it be fifteen years? My God, Joe, if I had a Volvo, I might never have met you.

When I think of the many miles we've traveled, I feel so lucky to have found you. Who else would know what I mean by "Driver-side door hinge sounds like my grandmother"?

My thanks for all your early-morning diagnostic work, on-the-money estimates, loving engine care and careful attention to my cars' brakes and fluids. And for the always mischievous smile that first plays, then breaks wide open, under your mustache.

This thank-you comes with a lifetime warranty.

Sincerely,

Pam J.

Dear unknown man from L.A. on TWA Flight #848 from JFK to Rome/Athens, September 22, 1989,

Well, I'd never really gotten motion sickness before, but then I'd never taken an eight-and-a-half-hour flight before, either, and that doesn't count the two-plus hours it took to get from National to JFK, including the ninety minutes of circling over Atlantic City during rush hour in New York.

So of course I missed my connection to Rome, as if the tension of meeting my then-boyfriend there weren't high enough already.

Have you ever been on a trip that seemed ill-fated from start to finish?

The airline put me on your flight because it was the next one leaving for Rome. The hot flashes began soon after. Then, when I asked, the flight attendants told me they didn't give out Dramamine—or anything else—because of possible lawsuits. (Thank you very much; I'll be sure to aim for you instead of the bag.)

The only way I could have felt worse was if I had known then what I found out in Rome: that creep had been with another woman in Paris the week before. Would you say the fates were trying to tell me something here?

I remember feeling horrible, putting ice cubes down the front of my blouse, realizing I was getting sicker by the minute, eyeing first the compact little bag in the seat pocket in front of me, then my watch, and thinking, "Oh, no, eight more *hours* . . ."

Then you appeared in the aisle next to me. Where did you come from? How was it that my head was up, not down, in that moment and we made eye contact?

"You're not feeling well, are you?" you said. "Would

you like some Dramamine? I know you're supposed to take it before you take off, but who knows—it might work anyway. I've been taking it since I left home in L.A. this morning."

"Yes, please," I said.

I was too miserable at the time to really thank you, and when I looked for you in the customs line in Rome, you were gone.

Anyway, the Dramamine worked, even at that eleventh hour. The relationship, as you can guess, didn't.

As it turned out, that was the inaugural flight of one of my yucky adult discoveries: without drugs on planes, I get terrible motion sickness. Dramamine: I don't leave home without it.

I should be thanking the Upjohn Co. (how apt)—and I do every time I board a plane; don't even talk to me about boats—but yours is the face I saw, briefly and blurrily, in my misery en route to further yucky adult discoveries.

There's nothing anyone can do about other people's crummy dating choices—call it emotion sickness—but at least there's relief for life's other up-and-down rides.

I always carry an extra supply of Dramamine when I fly now for others in need.

Whoever you are, thanks for coming to my first aid.

Sincerely,

Seat 32C

Thank you.

This afternoon I'd like to share my thoughts with you about one of my dearest friendships, a friendship that began with a professional speechwriting association.

It zoomed into girlfriend territory one frosty day in late 1985, when I commented on the apparent coziness of your coat and you said, quote, "No one wears a mink to keep warm."

You were the age I am now, the first woman everything in publishing it seemed, leaving out Katharine Graham. A Chicago girl in Washington via New York, you brimmed with the heartland's friendliness, the capital's confidence, and the city's energy.

I loved you the moment I met you. But you had a lot of work to do training me: "I won't say 'love' in a speech," you declared. "It's too . . . *pink*. A man wouldn't say it, and a woman who does won't be taken seriously."

You make the exception in commencement speeches, because your wish for young women and men to live full lives includes this heartfelt tenet: "Find someone to love."

You always write your own best lines, Cath.

(pause)

Thank you for being my mentor in both work and life. I'm not overstating when I say you've probably had the most lasting and indelible influence on my post–age-thirty years of anyone who's had a part in them.

I've learned the most from you not in how you run a profit center but in how you live a life.

One of your great gifts as a manager and as a friend is

your ability to blend all of life's joys and tasks into a whirl that would bring on vertigo in most people but just makes you more clearly and surely value each of them. I've never, ever heard you complain about being tired, even when you've crossed fourteen time zones and gotten home to discover that everyone, including the nanny, has the stomach flu. Your spirit is more contagious than a bug; by showing everyone in your life that happiness is thoroughly enjoying whatever it is one has, you make us all recognize the abundance in our own lives.

You've been a good friend to more people than you know, Cathie. Anyone who's asked me for advice in the last fifteen years has gotten yours. I've passed along your counsel and commentary to at least these many people: my sister Michele; my cousin Julianne; my mother; a couple of college seniors I met in a Paris bistro in 1990 who were angsting about the so-called Real World; my hairstylist, Debbie; the social worker sitting next to me in the window seat on a flight home from San Francisco who was contemplating a career change; my agent, Leslie; and countless friends.

Your insights on life, love and staff meetings have had more reruns than *M*A*S*H*.

Here are some of the life's lessons we all—and especially I—thank you for:

○ Move forward.

○ Assume nothing.

○ Dream big dreams.

○ Do what you love.

- Be grateful for everything in your life, including the curveballs, because any opportunity to grow is ultimately positive.

- Don't spend money on dinners out. Marry someone who cooks.

- Apply business smarts to life: set goals based on what you want the big picture to look like, plan responsibly to take risks, and focus your energy first where it's needed most.

- Apply life smarts to business: deal directly and straightforwardly with people, ask for help when you need it, and dress appropriately.

- Put people first. Cherish your family and friends; recognize and thank your employees.

- When feeling stuck, ask yourself, "Is anything about this [job, boss, relationship] going to change?" If the answer is no, see first bullet.

- Build a consensus before the meeting.

- Don't stress about leaving a job. They'll get over you. Quickly.

- Remember the people who opened doors for you by opening doors for others.

- Unwind with a few guests after every party.

- Write handwritten notes and send silly cards to your friends.

- Invite people over for dinner on the spur of the moment.

- Don't take late-night calls from men who have hurt you. ("Lose *more* sleep over him; what, are you kidding?")

- When dealing with devastating breakups, don't call in distraught. Go to the office, and—to quote you exactly from my little balled-up Kleenex session on the couch in your *USA Today* office that time—"Be grateful for the work, and don't cry in meetings."

(pause)

Thank you, Cathie, for all the wonderful, festive Christmas Eves that you've included me in (including the one I brought a boyfriend to; pointing the video camera at him, you said, "Wait, should I do this? Are you planning to be in the picture next year?" I almost hated to break up with him after that).

Thank you for making me an honorary Black/Harvey and sharing the gracious and irrepressible Tom—who cooks!—Duffy, Alison, Peg, all the sibs and Fred and Renee Priori with me.

Thanks for being the kind of friend a woman would gladly share her lipstick with.

Thank you for being warm and wise and for living days and years to their fullest and then some, knowing and showing how precious time is.

And thank you, Cathie, for helping me realize some of *my* big dreams.

Thank you.

Dear Lester and Rick,

I kept the Metro's Towing card you guys gave me when you rescued me on Connecticut Avenue one day, because I wanted to write you this note. The card's been in my Rolodex for a long time.

In case this hasn't happened to you a million times when you've been on your way to real tow jobs, I'm the woman who realized she'd locked her keys in her 1990 red Geo Prizm four-door hatchback just as rush hour started and parking there became illegal.

I was sure I'd see a cop with a ballpoint poised over a pink ticket pad before I'd ever see help. But then your truck turned onto Connecticut from K Street, and you saw me, stopped and asked if I needed a hand.

"Need some help?" are the some of the most welcome words we hardly ever hear.

Bless you for stopping and having the tools with you to do the job.

You wouldn't take any money, but I wanted to write to say thank you.

       Sincerely,

       Pam Janis

Dear Pammys I,

After years of being the only two Pams in my school classes (me and my inner child), I find you and *your* inner child. At a Fortune 500 company, of all places.

It *is* a New Age.

By the way, thanks for outdoing me in the inner-child-humor department. I told you I was leaving my job to stay home with mine, and you said you'd preboarded a plane with yours.

Thank you for three of my favorite books (different birthdays), *Women Who Run With the Wolves*, Mary Oliver's *New and Selected Poems*, and *How to Massage Your Cat*.

Thanks for coming over at eight-thirty that Saturday morning in August 1992 when I realized my left hand didn't work and that that made two, since the carpal tunnel had already crippled my right. You brought me a wrist brace, then stayed to make me breakfast, do all my dishes, open a few cans of cat food so Callie would be taken care of and generally console me. I don't know what I would have done without you that morning.

Thanks for sending cards and notes to say hi, or thanks, or thinking of you, or anything. I have some lovely and thoughtful messages from you in every room of my home. Thanks for being a friend who tends friendships like a garden.

I would be remiss as an evolving human being if I did not add a cosmic thank you for telling me to read *The Celestine Prophecy*, even though if I was truly destined to read it, somehow I would have heard of it or seen it even if you hadn't said anything to me.

Thanks for adding the catchphrase "What a hoot" to my life.

Thank you for all these things and for being one of my heroines in, as you put it, the "Hero's Work" that is life.

Love,

Pammys2

Dear Aunt Dotty,

I hope it's okay that I'm calling you "Aunt Dotty," even though you're Phil's aunt and not mine. It must be strange to hear from an ex-girlfriend of your nephew's, but he's the sort of guy who makes his ex-girlfriends—and all his other chums—want to know him and every important person in his life forever.

This could make for some very crowded family seders.

I'm writing to thank you for Phil. For giving him to the world, I mean. I know that technically he wasn't yours to give and I should be writing this letter to his parents, Lillian and Harold, and I do thank them, but I never knew them. Since you and Uncle Artie are the ones who stepped in when Phil was nine and Lillian died, I wanted to tell you how grateful all his friends are to you for giving him a sense of family that makes even his exes want to stay in his *mishpacha*, his family.

The first time I met you, the weekend your youngest graduated from college, Phil and I drove up to New Jersey to celebrate with you. I was so nervous but felt at home even before I got out of the car; Uncle Artie was waving from the doorstep: "Hello! I'm going to get the cake!" You welcomed me in with a hug that said, "So hello already! What took you thirty-three years?," a hug you give to everyone who comes into your home.

Thanks for making me feel so wonderful that weekend. Now back to Phil.

Your nephew is a person who makes fun happen wherever he goes, which is really saying something for a TV producer on a crime show. He works at nabbing America's most-wanted crooks and crazies, yet is so full of tenderness and love for the world, especially its children. He started the cousins singing group, Phil and the Phillettes, to showcase their talent (and his), which would have been entertaining enough to the world, but he then gave them this song when one of your granddaughters was three and fascinated with eyeballs:

> Put your eyeball in your ear, in your ear,
> Put your eyeball in your ear, in your ear,
> Put your eyeball in your ear so you can see
>   what you can hear,
> Put your eyeball in your ear, in your ear.

(In the second verse, you put your eyeball on your knee so you can see it while you ski.)

The world *needs* Phil.

He loves the Yankees, the Beatles and his guitar. He's a music maven; he knows every song lyric ever written and sings all of Bob Dylan's like Bob Dylan. He hosts the best New Year's Eve party in the Washington area. (The official Phil's New Year's Eve attire is always black and white—his friends are all running out of outfits.) You'll be in the middle of a conversation with him, probably at Chadwick's, on Wisconsin Avenue, and he'll suddenly look into your face and say, "*Nice* to see you."

Phil is the kind of man who reads James Thurber stories out loud to a sick girlfriend (that was me); who always has five kinds of candles on hand (romantic, dinner, Chanuka, power failure, and yahrzeit); and can't believe you've never seen *The Sunshine Boys*. He gets *verklempt* every time he rents *Field of Dreams*.

Everyone calls Phil for advice in the romance

department—and I'm not kidding, I mean *everyone,* including one of my boyfriends after Phil. (The boyfriend who, your nephew told me, all my friends liked better than *me.*) I'd broken up with the guy and he was upset, so he called . . . Phil. Phil's advice was "You'll get over her."

Then I met someone else who broke up with me, and *I* called Phil: "He likes make-up sex, but we never fight. He says I'm too nice."

"He doesn't think you're *meshugguneh* enough? Has he checked under the hood?"

"Should I just be myself?"

"That works for some people, but don't you be yourself."

"I hope you're not charging me for this therapy. Why shouldn't I be myself?"

"Because when people find themselves in emotional hurricanes, they tend to put on windbreakers."

"Thank you, O Delphic Oracle."

"A pleasure. Don't mention it."

The only time I ever beat him at GHOST was with the word "tomfoolery."

He makes the young reporters who work for him read the newspapers.

I haven't had a boyfriend since Phil with whom I could watch *A Hard Day's Night* knowing we'd both jump up from the couch during the songs, grab whatever was handy to use as a microphone, and one of us would be John, the other Paul.

He's a *guttinke,* a *mensch,* a man who makes his friends dinner. He always sets a lovely table.

If I didn't already know him, I'd want to meet him.

Don't even ask me why we broke up; there are so many different kinds of relationships two people can have, and "just friends" seems to work best for us. (My mother hates it when her daughters talk about "relationships"; she once zinged us with this riddle: "I never had a relationship. I was *married*.")

But Phil isn't "just" a friend to me or anyone else who knows him; he's beloved. I wanted to thank someone for its being so *nice* to see him in the world, and if I thanked him, he'd be insufferable.

So, Aunt Dotty, I'm thanking you.

Love,

The one from before he had the convertible

Dear Bruce Springsteen,

"Listen to this."

A guy I dated briefly, very, in college was playing a song called "Blinded by the Light" for me because he was sure I'd recognize your genius as he had.

I told him I didn't like it.

There was a pause as he assessed whether to continue knowing me.

"You're kidding," he said. "How can you not like this?"

"The guy's voice is too raspy," I complained. "I can't understand what he's saying. . . . *Cut loose like a* douche? *is* the what *in the night*?"

Nice knowing me.

I was a moron. Can you believe they let me graduate?

I thank my dear friend Vicki Barker for flicking the switch.

"Listen to this," she said, tipping an album called *Born to Run* out of its cover in our New York railroad flat as I noted with a sinking feeling that it was the douche guy's. "He wrote it in a house he rented from my parents."

Oh. Well. Someone who Mr. and Mrs. Barker knew was another story. Okay, I'll give Bruce Springsteen another try.

I'm writing to humbly beg your pardon, Mr. Springsteen, and to thank you—because I've been electrified by your music and poetry ever since.

(And let me here thank Mima—Ruth, Vicki's mother—and A.J.—Jim, Vicki's father—for having had that house in Atlantic Highlands, because otherwise I might have spent twenty-two more years thinking the Supremes were profound.)

I have wanted to write you this letter all these years.

First, thank you for your luminous, exuberant early music, which always lifts my heart to heights—and plunges it into depths—of feeling I sometimes forget I'm capable of. Your music cores me as you've cored the shouts and wails of Jersey girls and boys. The way you locate stories inside of images inside of words inside of music inside of notes inside of instruments blows me away all over again every time I hear one of your songs.

I remember one evening a few winters ago, when my ice skating buddy Mary Rumsey and I were skating late in the moonlight on Washington's Mall rink. It was close to 11 P.M.—closing time—and we two were the only skaters left on the ice, which was choppy after a session of end-of-day dull rental blades.

"Jungleland" came on, and I suddenly went wild on my skates, tearing around the rink's and music's curves, sailing through their centers as song and scene became one, racing and slowing between solid and wetter ice patches and music transitions, jumping in joy over holes in the ice as the music arched and vaulted—and then I realized: I'm not a good skater; Bruce Springsteen is making me do this.

"Boss," you make music with a poignancy and power like I've never heard.

Thank you for composing what you saw and knew in a way that makes us see and know it too. Like J. D. Salinger's, yours is a voice that yearning souls recognize as the one inside us, yet it belongs to you alone.

I owe you a special thank-you, because the restless shore life you put to music turned out to be my first reporting beat. At the now-defunct Red Bank *Daily Register* for the first two years of the '80s, I saw with my own eyes the things you'd already made come alive for me: the girls who combed their hair in rearview mirrors; the pinball wizards who played on the boardwalk way past dark; the cosmic kids in full costume dress. (Was there a Jungleland mini-golf place on the Long Branch boardwalk before Bruce Springsteen's mainstream breakthrough? I wondered.)

Every third new *Register* reporter, it seemed, wanted to knock on the door of the house in Freehold in which you grew up and interview the current beleaguered occupants, who quickly had enough of us and our rivals at *The Asbury Park Press*. We'd go to the Stone Pony, too, hoping it was one of the nights you'd be there as a surprise jammer. (It never was.)

Thanks for making it such a great time to be young in New Jersey. And for giving me, a non-native, such a strong feeling and affection for the place I began my adult life in.

Thanks for "Fire," "Because the Night," "Thunder Road," "Prove It All Night," "Hungry Heart," "Born in the U.S.A.," "My Hometown," "Philadelphia," and your version of "Santa Claus Is Coming to Town."

Thanks for your more recent music, your haunting, thoughtful ballads with their stark images, and your care and concern for the people whose lives and dreams you wrap so tenderly in them.

Thank you most of all for singing the soul's truest songs of dreams without despair, restlessness without rage, longing without lost hope, and fear always tempered with faith.

Since violence has become such a part of music, I've been listening to yours more to remind me that anger does its best work fueling dreams and plans for something better.

Thank you, Bruce, for being born to rock. I was blinded by the light.

Sincerely,

Pam Janis

P.S.: I have *never* been able to understand that *"Cut loose . . ."* line. Could you please tell me what it is?

"To Life! To Life! L'Chaim!
L'Chaim! L'Chaim! To Life!"

—FIDDLER ON THE ROOF

Dear Grandma Helen and Grandpa Max,

You were both legends to your family even while you
lived. And The Cousins, as cousin Elaine calls your
fourteen grandchildren, are still telling the stories.

There was, to begin with, the fact that neither of you
had been born in America, the way all of us had; you
came here on big boats.

You came to America—and you always called it
America, never the United States or the U.S.A., which
made it an almost mythical place for us, too—from
different countries at different times, on different ships at
different ages. Same class, though: steerage. (Grandpa Max
used to say he traveled third class because there was no
fourth class.) My mother, your daughter Lucille, painted
such a vivid picture of your seasickness that I will never in
this lifetime set foot on even a so-called "pleasure cruise."
("Never say never," mystical—and practical—Grandma
Helen would say. "Nobody knows what tomorrow has
waiting.")

Grandpa Max was fourteen when he came from Poland,
from a little town named Dobrzyn (pronounced *Dubjin*)
near the German border. Grandma Helen's little town, Zetl,
(pronounced *Jetel*), was sometimes Russian, sometimes
Polish, depending on who'd won the latest border war.
Your American story and my thank-yous start with the
boats that took you away from them long, long ago.

Grandpa Max, as the tale goes, made the passage to
America alone in 1913, a boy whose family launched him,
as countless other families launched their young hopes, "to
a better life." His father, already in America with Grandpa's

older sister, Ida, had worked for the money to send for him.

While Grandpa waited for his father and sister at Ellis Island, he got bored and wanted to buy an entertainment—a snack, a Hebrew newspaper, who knows what. So he asked to borrow some money from a man on his ship who spoke his language; his father, he said, would pay him back when he got there. The man gave him a dollar from his own pocket ("How did a man on Grandpa's boat happen to have an American dollar?"—"Who knew?"). But then Grandpa Max spotted his family and lost sight of the man in the crowd.

Twenty-six years later, in 1939, Grandpa, by then a prosperous Garment District *macher* with his own belt-and-button factory, was crossing Seventh Avenue at Thirty-eighth Street one day when he looked up, and there, crossing the same street from the opposite corner, was a familiar face. He met the man halfway and walked with him back to the corner he'd just stepped from (a good thing; the guy might have had a heart attack in the middle of traffic when he heard this).

"Mister," Grandpa Max said, "I owe you a dollar."

"True story!" (I've heard these words so many times in my life from my mother, Aunt Bernice, Aunt Harriet and Uncle Herbie that I don't even pretend I'm a post–Watergate reporter around them anymore. What's the point?)

So first, thank you, Grandpa Max, for passing along your good memory to me when the Goldfeder genes were dealt. Mine isn't as good as yours was (no one's is), but it comes in handy when my reporting skills *are* called for.

(Also in the silly genetic accidents department, thank

you for good teeth. Every dentist I've gone to in my life, it seems, compliments me on mine, usually while my mouth is full of the dental paraphernalia that kept you in toothpicks and out of dentists' chairs your whole life. I've got to hand it to you: you may have thought toothpaste was a waste of time and money and floss was cousin Loretta's married name, but you had the best teeth in the family—and all of them, to boot, when you died. I will never understand this.)

You were a man who loved a commotion, or *tumul* in Yiddish, especially when you were at its center. When the whole family got together, the decibel level was somewhere between the sirens of the police cars careening down the Grand Concourse and the roar of a summer Saturday at Yankee Stadium a few blocks away. You and Grandma moved apartments twice while I was growing up, but never farther away than a different route's walk to the shul. Since you were always within earshot of Bronx *tumul* anyway, by the time the *kinder* finally got to you, we were *ubgaluhzim vildechaias* (out-of-control wild natives), gassy, stuffed like *kishkes* with Grandma Helen's chicken soup and kreplach (or borscht with sour cream, depending on the season and whether the meal was *milchich* or *fleishich*, milk or meat), chopped liver, gefilte fish, Jewish rye bread, challah, kasha varnishkes, lokshen kugel, farfel, blintzes, knishes, varied cuts of boiled kosher beef, roast chicken, Mogen David salami . . . "Here's the green vegetable," my dad would say as the pickles, sour and half sour, would be borne in on a platter . . . all this would roll out of Grandma's small galley kitchen until the adults were moaning, my father asking where the Eno antacid was, and the *kinder* were shrieking, chasing one another around the apartment in one group meltdown; then, you, Grandpa Max, would pronounce the main course over to Grandma Helen: *"Enough with the food, already."*

The meal officially adjourned for a short break while Grandma cleared and reset the plates like bowling pins for dessert. She and her daughters would set out honey cakes, macaroons, fancy bakery cakes with roses made from frosting, and cookies with maraschino cherry and jelly centers, stewed prunes and apricots, nuts in their shells, hard fruit-flavored and soft butterscotch wrapped candies from their three-tiered glass dish on the coffee table in the living room that was filled with plastic-covered furniture, Jaffa oranges and enough glass bottles of soda to start a recycling center today. I was a tea drinker; thanks for that good ReaLemon stuff you always had.

"I want the rose!" all girl cousins present would shout near the cake, because we forgot from one time to the next how awful the sugary bloom always tasted, especially if it was blue.

With the *kinder* topped off with sugar and/or caffeine, it finally happened: someone made someone else cry. (Once it was my father saying to Elaine, who was then about eight—The Cousins were skipping around the table— "Why are *you* such a happy jalappy?" That did it; everyone broke loose, cousins and attending parents alike, while my father sat as far back as you can sit in a straight chair and said, confused, to no one in particular, *"What did I say?"*)

You, Grandpa Max, presided over the whole *gonsa tumul*, as well as the packing of the big glass jars and brown paper food bags for take-home in the way backs of station wagons. (My father to my mother, ten minutes on the Major Deegan Expressway as the smell of something Jewish began to fill the Dodge Dart: "What's leaking?")

Now, I will tell you this honestly, Grandpa Max: I can't remember a single conversation I ever had alone with you, or one that wasn't about how my Hebrew class was. Even when it was just the Janis children, those Reform-school miscreants who would, no doubt, have *bat* mitzvahs in a temple that wasn't a shul, where the *ubgaluhzim* men sat among women, half of them not even wearing yarmulkes.

No, I couldn't talk with you, Grandpa Max, not like Seth, the oldest cousin and the only boy for the longest time, who could read Hebrew without faking it. For one thing, you didn't like the Brownie uniform I was so proud of. What kind of business was this, dressing *kinder* like Nazis?

You were my most "foreign" grandparent (today we'd say "ethnic"), with your heavily accented Yiddish-English, Orthodox Jewish ways and the cultural canyon between us. But what awe you evoked in me when you took The Cousins to your shul, where Seth went with the men. How impressed I was when we went to the meetings of your Dobrzyn Young Men's Benevolent Society, the social group formed in New York by all the men who'd come to America from Dobrzyn for a better life. They called themselves *lontsmen,* men from the same land. We saw those men, your *lontsmen,* and men in suits from the UJA, too, honor you as an important *macher* for the Jews. I have a picture of you with the president of Israel himself, Mr. David Ben-Gurion, from the time you went to Tel Aviv in 1952 to see him on behalf, I thought, of all the Jews in America.

How you got Grandma on another boat with her

seasickness track record, I'll never know, but you sailed together to Israel in 1957. I know that because you were there when I had my first birthday that August. In my family memory book is a yellowed, important-looking piece of paper with a message spelled out in capital letters that you sent to me all the way from Jaffa that day. Your telegram said:

HAPPY BIRTHDAY PAMELA GRAND PARENTS=
GOLDFEDER=

Thank you for that bridge between your two worlds, Grandpa Max. Thank you for always connecting the generations and families you headed. Our parents turned into your *kinder* again at your house; the ones who'd married Goldfeders became polite guests. You ran the show, and it was a show of respect to one's religion and one's history. Had you been more Americanized ("assimilated," our parents called it), had you been a Gramps who disobeyed the *Shabbos* laws to take the *kinder* to the baseball games that clogged the traffic on the way to your house, I wouldn't have nearly as sure a sense of where I come from or cherish it so much.

Thank you, Grandpa Max, for giving me the gifts of understanding and being proud of my heritage. You gave those gifts as surely as you slipped all the *kinder* Olympic Belt & Button Co. pencils and dollar bills from your own pocket. What I owe you after forty years can't even be added up.

I can't imagine what it was like for you to see a girl on the *bima* for the first time, reading from the Torah, following the lines on the sacred parchment with the tip of her right index finger. And yet you were beaming at Temple Sinai when I read:

Vah yikrah Mosheh Lehoshua . . .

And Moses called to Joshua.

Thank you for coming to my bat mitzvah—and for being proud of me.

And thank you, Grandpa Max, for staying overnight that Shabbos Eve, even though you could never sleep in Connecticut because, you said, it was too quiet.

"I miss Mammaleh."

Cousin Julianne said this just the other night, the second seder of Passover this year, when eight of The Cousins assembled at Aunt Bernice and Uncle Howard's with their spouses, children, significant others, and in my case, cat hair. (I know you never liked it when animals lived in houses that were meant for people, Grandma Helen, but maybe you'd like my having a cat better than my having ferrets, which you thought was *meshuggeneh* altogether. Who, you asked me once when you were visiting my apartment, would marry a woman who kisses rats? They're *weasels*, I said. You looked into my bedroom, then said, "You let the *veesils* on your bed?")

I always miss you most at Passover; it still doesn't really feel like Pesach without you. It's been eight years now since you died in May; you'd made and frozen so much food for the seder at Aunt Bernice's only weeks before that we had it for Rosh Hashanah too.

What a strange and yet somehow comforting thing that was, to be eating the food you'd made for us, five months after you'd died. You were gone, but your horseradish lingered. ("Jewish Dristan" was my father's name for it.)

I miss your gefilte fish, Grandma Helen, and I don't even like gefilte fish. Thanks for the schools of it you made for us over the years.

The Bernstein girls all called you and Grandpa Mammaleh and Papa Max. My father called you Hindelaya, your Hebrew name. Your daughters called you Mom; Uncle Herbie called you Grandma, too, when The Cousins were around. Grandpa called you "Hey," which drove you *meshuggeneh* ("What does he think, I'm a horse?"), and your neighbors in the Concourse Village apartment complex called you Mrs. Goldfeder and asked which grandchild you were with.

"Pemela," you'd introduce me as. "Lucille's oldest."

It was mostly your women friends who called you Helen, some of whom you'd known since you arrived in New York on the S.S. *Mount Carroll,* November 14, 1922. You were sixteen years old.

I remember the story of how, twelve days of herring and black bread after the ship set sail from Hamburg, as it powered closer and closer to New York Harbor, the ship people told the new immigrants that the next day's dawn would bring America. Some *chuchem* from Zetl had told the town they'd see a big statue of Columbus holding a torch when they got there, so they had to explain to you it wasn't Columbus. The next day at 6 A.M., you scrambled to the deck, and it wasn't long before the shouts of joy went up. By then you knew what it was you were seeing.

"It was America," you said, telling the story. "The Stetue of Liberty."

You, Grandma Helen, you who had seen Zetl smashed

to the ground and set fire to by the Cossacks from the window of your family's house with the dirt floor and straw roof; you who were all of six when you first heard shooting and howling and moaning and then more shots and then saw the dead bodies of your *londsmen*; you who weren't supposed to be the next in line in your family to come to America at all, but then your older sister, Minnie, wouldn't go, because she wanted to get married there— Minnie, who saw three of her own children shot and killed by Cossacks before she, too, came to America. But it was you who came first for a better life, and so it was you and not Minnie who saw the Statue of Liberty on that almost-winter morning. You were so grateful to see the Lady's torch that you voted in every single U.S. election from when you became a citizen in 1927 to the year you died, 1990. You did that, you said, because you *could*. And you were there when the New York polls opened at 6 A.M., the same hour you first saw America, standing up to the Cossacks.

Thank you, Grandma Helen, for making me a loyal U.S. and District of Columbia voter even in the years when, as you might say, you want to hold your nose from the whole thing.

Now I'll tell *you* a story about the Statue of Liberty. Remember that boy I knew at Columbia? The one who was always in the library? (I tried to explain to you that he was busy in the library instead of asking me to marry him because he was getting his Ph.D. You said, "Tell him he can't sleep with books.")

Well, one night that year for some reason or no reason—I can't remember anymore (I'm very selective about how I use Grandpa's memory in the boyfriend department)—I was moved to ride the Staten Island Ferry and asked him to come along. He was studying, of course, but I really wanted to go, so he put down his yellow highlighter and shut his book, and off we went on the Broadway–Seventh Avenue local to the Battery and New York Harbor. It was a beautiful, warm spring night, dark enough to see the moon and stars clearly and hear the water lapping at the sides of the boat. I was having a nice time and wasn't nauseous.

Anyway, the Statue of Liberty came into view. I thought of you and the first time you saw it and what it meant to you, and I felt *verklempt*. So I turned to my boyfriend and said something to open your story like, "I always think of my Grandma Helen when I see the Statue of Liberty." And this *chuchem* said to me, "Really? I always think of the French Revolution and how they did theirs so much better than we did ours."

That's when I realized that we were, you should pardon the expression, two ships passing in the night. So I thank you for saving *me* from sleeping with books.

When I started wondering how it was that two people who happened to meet each other fell in love and decided to get married, I asked my mother how you and Grandpa Max met. (This was around the time of the big news that Paul McCartney was marrying some girl named Linda—an American! So it *could* have been me.)

I was assuming two things, of course, like all '60s girls who watched *He and She,* and *Bridget Loves Bernie* on TV: that every marriage began with a love story and every love story ended with a marriage. (Wait, that came out wrong.) My mother set me straight.

"The matchmaker gave them two marriages for fifteen dollars," she began.

"WHAT?!"

True story: Before Grandpa Max, you were married to a *londsman* from Zetl who was killed in a construction accident when Aunt Harriet was very little. Grandpa Max—now, this is a story altogether, my mother said—had been married to another woman from whom he got a *get* (there was such a thing as a Jewish divorce?; this was news to me). Uncle Herbie was little too. So you and Grandpa both went to a matchmaker in Brooklyn looking for a father for Aunt Harriet and a mother for Uncle Herbie, respectively. The matchmaker, Shotkin Rubin, made the match for ten dollars. ("It was a Shotkin wedding," you'd say later.) Evidently, hitting it off on your first date—except it was called an "appointment," not a date—you decided to meet again, only this time you brought along your niece Jean, and Grandpa brought his brother Milton. When Jean and Milton got married, too, Shotkin Rubin got mad, thinking he deserved another ten dollars, for *them*.

The case was settled two for fifteen dollars.

"And so from then on, my aunt Jean was Grandma Helen's niece and sister-in-law," my mother finished. "And Uncle Milton called her Helen and Tante Helen both, and Grandpa was Milton's brother and uncle."

(And so to bed. Why, *why*, was my family so wacky?, I wondered. Everyone else's family stories ended with ". . . And they lived happily ever after. . . ." Or so I thought at the time.)

So I learned from you that relationships are always more complicated than they appear to be. Also, that you have to share goals to make a marriage work, let alone make it last. Also, that you are absolutely right: Nobody knows what tomorrow has waiting.

You had a Yiddish saying for this, *"Menschen tracht, Gott lacht,"* or "Man plans, God laughs."

Thank you for all these life's lessons.

But one thing bothered me for a long time anyway:

"Do Grandpa Max and Grandma Helen love each other?," I'd ask my mother. "Of course," she'd say, but I was a post–Watergate reporter in training years before Watergate.

"It doesn't make sense to me," I'd tell her. "The marriage was so practical. How could they?" She'd look at me like I was my father's child.

So she explained it this way: in Grandma's day, when a good provider married a good mother who made a good home, that was a good marriage.

You and Grandpa Max always reminded me of that great song from *Fiddler on the Roof*, "Do You Love Me?" Tevye and Golde were fixed up by the town matchmaker but saw their daughters marrying for love. So Tevye asks Golde, *"Do you love me?"*

"I'm your wife."

"I know, But do you love me?"

"Do I love him? For twenty-five years I've lived with him, fought with him, starved with him, twenty-five years my bed is his. If that's not love, what is?"

"Then you love me?"

"I suppose I do."

"And I suppose I love you too."

Thanks, Grandma Helen, for showing me that there are different kinds of love stories.

Yours and Grandpa Max's lasted fifty-three years.

*　　*　　*

Thanks to you, I ended up in Washington, D.C.

I wish I could say it's because you loved America and freedom so much that you inspired me to live in its epicenter. The truth is, I lost a tooth when I was eight, and the Tooth Fairy, speaking through my mother, said, "How would you like to go to Washington with Grandma Helen to visit Aunt Bernice and Uncle Howard and The [Bernstein] Cousins?"

You took me on the biggest adventure of my life thus far.

We got up early on the first day of my school vacation to take the subway from the Bronx to the Port Authority in Manhattan, and then a Greyhound bus all the long way to Washington. Aunt Bernice picked us up and took us home to Maryland.

Thank you for taking me to see the cherry blossoms for the first time, Grandma Helen.

I don't know whether it was the trees that looked like cotton candy or the big, big houses with the flags on Massachusetts Avenue or the fact that there was a long street named Connecticut Avenue just like where I was from, but the fact is, I got bitten by the Washington bug on my Tooth Fairy trip here with you, Grandma, years before reading Allen Drury's novel *Advise and Consent* sealed the deal for me.

It makes me laugh to this day to think that the two things I remember most about that week are staying up late talking to my cousin Ellen for hours after we were supposed to be asleep, and Aunt Bernice showing us everything in Washington, D.C. Because, as you knew before you died, Ellen and I did the same thing a dozen years later when we lived in the same house at Smith, and Aunt Bernice now runs a tour company here for out-of-town visitors. The only difference now is that they tend to come with their convention colleagues, instead of their grandmas.

Thank you for bringing me to discover my future home.

It's also you I have to thank for my good skin and my, shall we call it, occasionally irreverent eye on life. I get hysterical when I think of you saying, at a wedding of an already much-married relative, as the glass shattered under his heel, "He's broken already a whole set of dishes."

Or, after Grandpa Max's strokes, when he was almost completely disabled and losing his incredible memory, and you were struggling to care for him in your last apartment in Brighton Beach, what you told my mother: "Such fights I had with his sisters to marry him. If they still want him, they can have him back now."

"You have no children?" you said to a new senior center acquaintance with whom you were playing cards. "What do you do for eggrevation?"

The year before you died, you had a pair of boots that made you look as rebellious as a teenager. No one could mess with you when you wore them, you said. You called them your "Goddemmit boots." (Thanks for posing for that picture in them; it lives on my dresser. Julianne's too.)

How you could make me laugh, Grandma Helen, you who'd seen such terrible things as a little girl in Zetl and were so seasick on your way to see Columbus; you who lost a young husband and cared for an old one. How you could see life's humor before its heartache makes about as much sense to me as how Grandpa's teeth could be so good, but I guess you figured that if God laughs, we all might as well too.

Thank you for giving me such a standard of resilience, courage and faith to live up to.

When you were in Suburban Hospital in Bethesda after the first of the two heart attacks that eventually took you, you made me tell you a secret about a boy I knew. But I made you sign a piece of paper first, swearing you'd never tell anyone, because I knew my mother would love to know it, too, and I'd never hear the end of it if she did. So I went running to the nurses' station for a scrap of paper and a pencil and, giggling with you in the ICU like one of The Cousins, commanded you to affix your signature to the back of one Tillie Billman's urinalysis report.

I know what the paper was, because I always carry it, with your signature and your sworn declaration ("I WILL NOT TELL PAMELA'S SECRET") around with me in my wallet. Thanks for that treasure.

And I will never tell my mother what it was you signed, either.

But I should never say never; nobody knows what tomorrow has waiting.

Thank you, Grandma Helen and Grandpa Max, for being the brave teenagers you were to board boats to America for a better life, and for working so hard to make a good life for so many others when you got here, including your oldest granddaughter, me.

Love,

Pamela

*   *   *

P.S.: Thanks, too, to The Cousins, all thirteen of you, for
the fun you brought when we came together as *kinder*, and
for the fun and memories you bring when we come
together as adults.

Dear Gregory, Shoshi, Everett, Annie, Katie C, Matthew, Halle, Skyler, Sarah, Emily, Ned, Katie M., Xander, Ellen and Alisia,

Thanks for being the kids in my life (or, in Sarah and Alisia's case, the almost-teens) and for being such good friends to me. You all live in different places, but you have one thing in common: you're very important to me, and I love you! Whether you call me Aunt Pam, Pam, Toots, Miss Pam, or Pam Janis (how did fifteeen people come to call me five different names?), I feel lucky to know you.

There's a lot of stuff I could say about everyone, but then you'd all call to tell me what I left out.

Since I don't have any children of my own (although you know how much I *love* my cat, Callie), I'm happy × 15 to have all of you to remind me how different and interesting the world looks when you first discover everything in it.

Whenever I play or talk with you, I always learn something new from and about each one of you. Some of the things you taught me about are:

1) holding, feeding and bathing babies—and changing their diapers
2) dinosaurs
3) Barbies
4) all sports
5) *Horton Hears a Who*
6) gargoyles
7) dollhouses
8) art
9) *The Simpsons*
10) Hanson

*   *   *

So maybe you can see why I'm thankful to have you all in my life. For all those fun things (okay, *not* changing diapers), plus the way you show me how important sharing, thoughtfulness, and being kind to people are.

Thank you, Greggy, Shoshi, Everett, Annie, Katie C., Matthew, Halle, Skyler, Sarah, Emily, Ned, Katie M., Xander, Ellen, and Alisia, for brightening my life like the sun that always rises no matter how many times you say Goodnight Moon.

Love,

Whatever you call me

Dear Jan,

I once read an interview with Woody Allen—in the
'70s, I think it was—in which he said that when he
discovered Diane Keaton, he wanted to introduce her to
the world. That's the way I feel about you.

World, meet Janet Lee Cochenour Emmons Johnson,
Jan for short.

As many parents as I've heard in hospital corridors
thank you for being a friend to their children with cancer,
I've yet to thank you for opening up your life to me and,
in so doing, opening my heart to sick kids. I don't know
anyone else who can evoke, in a new recruit to your
cause, empathy and hilarity at the same time—or, in kids
both sick and healthy, just hilarity. You're like the Pied
Piper, compelling people to donate time, money and caring
to "your" kids, all the while being followed by a dozen of
them, some bald from chemo, some wearing catheters,
some dragging Broviacs, and all of them having the time of
their lives.

How many times in your capers as Sunrise the Clown
has a defeated parent said to you in wonder, "You're the
only one who got a smile out of her today"? Who else
would have pestered Paula Abdul's managers/handlers/
surround-abouts ad nauseam for some message from her to
grant the wish of a dying teen named Todd, realize time
was running out, send a telegram yourself from "Paula
Abdul" to her "#1 Fan," then watch in amazement as
signed letters, cards, tapes and posters poured in to Todd
from the *real* Paula Abdul?

Who else would rush to a little girl's oxygen tent at two
in the morning with her favorite raccoon puppet after her

mom called to say she was in and out of a coma, and be greeted by rice paper–thin fluttering eyelids and the words "My clown"?

Or would grant two sick kids' wishes at her own wedding by making one her flower girl and having the Baltimore Orioles mascot bird show up at the reception with cool Cal Ripken–signed stuff for the other?

Face it: you're amazing, a Baltimore-to-Washington treasure. And everything you do is on your own time and your own receptionist's salary, except for the donations from people who hear about you and *have* to get involved. It's hard to believe that you started your life's work, as you call it, with nothing but your mouth and the conviction that God was trying to tell you something by taking away so many of your own family members and friends via cancer.

I'm blown away all over again every time I think of your story: more than a dozen family members, including your mom, and close friends lost to cancer in little more than twenty years. Everyone who knows you agrees it's spooky; you yourself greeted me for the first time with this cheerful hello: "How's your health? Some people get nervous when they meet me."

You couldn't stop there, though. The rest of your welcome went like this (I was interviewing you, remember?—I kept the tape!): "Hello, you've reached Maryland's professional wailer. . . . If your death was in January, push one now. If your death was in February, push two now. If you're deciding when to die, you might try October; I don't have any days taken there yet."

(At this point in the tape, your friend Terry Powell, whose sister, your best friend Pat Needle, died of breast cancer in 1989, laughs so hard she covers whatever came next. I was thinking, Is this Jan person from *The Far Side,* or what?)

Who would have thought my "interview" five years ago with a "cancer activist" for a book I wanted to write on "transcenders"—people who have transcended adversity— would turn me into one of the Pied Piper's mesmerized rats?

The fact that you were willing to talk to a writer at all was astonishing. It was four weeks since your husband, Paul Emmons, died suddenly at thirty-nine from a brain aneurysm. I'd gone fishing for "transcenders" through my media contacts; a producer at Channel 9 in Washington told me about you but warned that you might not be "ready." I called you, hoping you'd keep me in mind for a chat about your life in six months, maybe a year. You invited me over that weekend.

You explained the unexpected hospitality by saying you'd been praying for a way to use your grief over Paul's death to continue helping other people, just as you've used cancer and your father's alcoholism as means to take meaningful action in the world, to be in service.

As I've come to know, that prayer to put troubles to work for others was pure Jan. Making a difference in someone else's life is what counts, you say. Anger in your own is useless and self-destructive. There are people out there, you say, who need *your* help, whoever you are.

The ways you've helped have been, as the kids say, "awesome":

Once when a pair of dejected parents asked you how to deal with the stares and questions directed toward their chemo-bald toddler, you said, "Just tell 'em she's Kojak's daughter."

In a visit with the healthy, frightened siblings of an eight-year-old newly diagnosed with cancer, you got them started on an ongoing art and journal project, describing what it's like to have a brother with cancer, that could help other kids going through the same thing.

You once got a Maryland mayor to declare a day honoring a child who'd had a bone-marrow transplant, threw a party and flew in a "special mystery guest"—the bone-marrow donor—from Minnesota via private plane donated by an anonymous backer of yours.

You're on call twenty-four hours; running a foundation, mountain retreat and countless birthday parties; making field trips with the kids and holiday visits, all after work and on weekends.

Rusty Gray, mother of Todd Paulus, Paula Abdul's "#1 Fan," told me when I was first getting to know you, "Being the parent of a child with cancer is a sad situation, an unbearable situation. You practically live in the hospital, and for the kids, it's like living in a pet store. . . .

"I saw Jan do miraculous things at the hospital. . . . She'd stick notes to the glass window that isolated the bone-marrow kids. She advised one mother to take down a picture of her bald daughter when she had long hair. She sometimes signed in the register as 'Aunt' to all the kids when it was family members only. She told us parents, 'I know I'm pushy, but unless you are, nobody's gonna give. You have to say, "This is my situation; I want you to help me" ' . . .

"I know her story and, frankly, I don't know how she does it. So many people fall down and stay down. She just gets right back up. You can grow to hate everything—kids, animals, everything. Not Jan."

"Even my *dog* died of cancer," you told me that first afternoon, laughing. "Petey. He was a Sheltie."

"Look," you said, "God and I . . . It's like we had this talk. It was like, okay, you've got two choices: You can be on your tail and feel sorry for yourself. You'll be alone if you do that. Or you can do something. When people have adversity in their life, they have *choices*. They can become a blob or turn negatives into positives. They can make hard times worse or make a difference. It's *that* easy. You have it in your soul."

I can't thank you enough for what you've taught me— just by living it—about first taking life as it comes, then taking action. And about resiliency: when, a year or two after Paul's death, a blind date showed up wearing the same shirt you'd buried Paul in, you rallied as usual. When you got done laughing, you placed a personal ad in your community newspaper and Pied Pipered Wayne Johnson down the aisle.

But mostly, thanks for enfolding me in your circle of fun and love. Thanks for giving me the gift of experiencing the delight of those little guys and dolls as you paint their faces, lead sing-alongs, and twist balloons into dogs that bark even in "Quiet Zones."

As Rusty Gray says, "There aren't enough thank-yous for people like Jan."

Here's mine anyway.

Love

Pammy

Dear Senator McGovern,

Hearing your voice when I interviewed you by phone to write about your book *Terry,* was at first an eerie experience; it was a voice at once so familiar and so new.

By the end of the call (and later our lunch, thank you!), I felt as though I knew you—and not only for what you've stood for and accomplished as a politician and statesman.

To even write a book subtitled *My Daughter's Life-and-Death Struggle with Alcoholism* takes such a degree of courage and conviction to serve—in this case, as you told me, other families engaged in that struggle—that I can only tell you how much I admire those qualities in you.

Nobody really thinks of politicians as being fathers and husbands, despite (or maybe because of) their "spinmeisters' " efforts to paint all the right pictures and deliver those hollow substitutes for heartfelt songs, "message points." Every image I have of a current political figure is just that—an image. One way or the other.

But by being Terry's dad (and Ann's, Sue's, Steve's and Mary's) and Eleanor's husband, you've shared so much more with *Terry*'s readers—and me—than a history lesson.

Thank you, Senator, for the reminder that life and families come with no guarantees—no matter who you are—and that the voices which most effectively speak out against wars of all kinds are our most compassionate.

Sincerely,

Pam Janis

Dear Lucky,

Just your luck to have meandered into the Haight in
San Francisco one day in the summer of 1993 and run
into those two women with the kid, neither of whom
would give you the five bucks you asked for. In fact, they
got so nervous around you, they asked you to leave.

The one with the kid, whose name is Matthew, was my
friend Toots. As you knew, we were in the street in front
of her house, looking for my earring. Do you remember?
The silver cat earring? The one I told you was so special
to me, because I'd gotten it the same day I got my cat?

You were very sly not to have told us right away that
you'd found it there at dawn, put it in your pocket and
come back when you'd seen us out there searching for it.
Also to have let us act unfriendly and bothered by you
because you were a homeless man.

I can't believe you didn't move on out of spite. After
all, we never would have known you had the earring.

We couldn't figure out why you hung around, even
after we'd told you to get lost, just watching us with that
smile on your face. Finally you said to me, your three gold
teeth showing, "I bet you're looking for an earrin', and I
can help you find it, 'cause I'm Lucky. That's what all the
Caucasians call me."

"Yeah, right," I said.

"What'll you give me if I find that earrin' for you?"

"A handshake," Toots interjected.

"You don't think I can, do you? Well, what if I told
you I found that earrin' already?"

I know I looked at you like you'd just flown in from
Mars.

But into your right pants pocket went your hand, and out came the earring.

The grin on your face was a sight to see. So, probably, was the grin on mine. Remember how we laughed and laughed?

That kindness was worth way more than five bucks, Lucky.

Thank you from the bottom of my momentarily urban-hardened heart for playing Toots and me like first violins.

Also, for my earrin'.

Love,

Pam Janis

TO: HANS CHRISTIAN ANDERSEN   D. H. LAWRENCE

      JANE AUSTEN   MARY MCCARTHY

      THE BRONTË SISTERS   TONI MORRISON

      CHARLES DICKENS   FAYE MOSKOWITZ

      THEODORE DREISER   GEORGE ORWELL

      GEORGE ELIOT   J. D. SALINGER

      NORA EPHRON   WILLIAM SHAKESPEARE

      O. HENRY   JEAN SHEPHERD

      VICTOR HUGO   AMY TAN

      SHIRLEY JACKSON   MARK TWAIN

      ERICA JONG   ANNE TYLER

      SUE KAUFMAN   EDITH WHARTON

      GARRISON KEILLOR   THOMAS WOLFE

      BARBARA KINGSOLVER   TOM WOLFE

      MAXINE HONG KINGSTON

Dear Friends I Don't Know,

Thank you for the wonderful stories that live on my shelves and in my heart. I return to them again and again to appreciate the brilliance with which you've crafted them. Always your rapt audience—as many times as I've read some of your works before—I feel moved, uplifted, entertained, understood, happy, amused, contemplative, stirred up, calmed down, darkened, lightened, reverent, irreverent, hopeful about the human condition, convinced we're all going to hell, then hopeful once more.

The wonder of language is its versatility: just as all music is composed of countless rearrangements of the same notes, your marvelous books are recombinations of the same words. Incredible that you all began with the most elementary of writing tools—a vocabulary—and produced *Pride and Prejudice,* "The Last Leaf," *Fear of Flying, King Lear, Dinner at the Homesick Restaurant, David Copperfield,* and "Wanda Hickey's Night of Golden Memories."

For your imaginations, ingenuity, innocence and illusions lost, insights and illuminations gained, I thank you from the bottom of my story-loving and -laden heart.

Most sincerely,

Pam Janis

P.S. *Your Cat Is Dead,* by James Kirkwood, is a favorite of mine.

Dear BiC,

Thank you for all the pens that I've used since I went
from #2 pencils (was there any other kind?) to ink,
sometime around the fourth grade. Fourth grade was a big
year, generally speaking—mostly for the white go-go boots
my parents finally let me have, with the money Grandma
Helen sent me—so I'm pretty sure that's when I grasped
my first BiC ballpoint pen.

Blue, medium point, that's me. The fine points make
my handwriting look and feel scratchy, but the medium
points glide right across the page, especially if there's more
paper under it. Red's good for corrections. I've tried to like
black, telling myself it's "me," because I wear a lot of it,
but for some reason blue always looks better to me on a
yellow legal pad or in a reporter's notebook. Green?
Christmas cards only, please.

I went through a cartridge pen phase in junior high
and still like the concept, but it's kind of messy if you're
the kind of writer I was back then, a fast and furious
scribbler. I couldn't pen the words onto my notes to
Helene Liebowitz fast enough.

Elegant gold and silver pens to dazzle colleagues and
clients in meetings? Lost 'em. As gone as sunglasses in a
rental car.

My computer? It has its place, but it just doesn't fit into
my purse.

There's just nothing like a medium-point BiC blue.
Even after college, I bought them one at a time, thinking
I'd be more likely to keep one long enough to use it up if
another wasn't waiting in the wings. Of course, when you
buy your pens one by one, you hope you're not getting a

lemon: one that inexplicably makes the ink gunk up and sends you running for tissues.

I buy my BiCs by the dozen now and have several standing by when I do interviews, should one falter or gunk up. A medium-point blue BiC is my personal leveler: I've written down the words of children and seniors, the filthy and filthy rich, unknowns and celebrities, with the same pen.

Thank you for enabling me to write the uncountable number of book reports, stories, essays, spelling tests, school and job applications, college lecture notes, roommates' phone messages, blue-book exams, postcards, Post-its, checks, credit card receipts, Christmas and birthday cards, Valentines, love letters, post-breakup analyses, reporting notes, interview notes, staff meeting notes, speeches, story contracts, 1040s, doctors' office and insurance forms, household budgets, grocery lists, "Things To Do," "I'm-sorrys" and "Thank-yous"—including the one to Grandma Helen for the go-go boots—that I've written, scrawled, scribbled, jotted, transcribed and signed through the years.

This thank-you is for the medium-point blue BiC. Thanks for making and selling the plastic ink-filled cylinders that have helped me write, if not a novel, a great American life.

Sincerely,

Pam Janis

Dear Veronica Parke, Olivia Ivy, and all the other wonderful people at Martha's Table,

Washington, D.C., can be an absurd, obnoxious place to live: its plethora of pretentious, self-important political wanna-bes; its partisan political I-ams; its hapless city government and taxpayer-be-warned faulty public services; its potholes; its crime; its falling-apart schools; its decapitated parking meters; its congressional naming of an airport for the president who fired all the air-traffic controllers; its warm embrace of the well-heeled, and chilly heart toward the no-soled, which is to say, a fair number of the people who actually live here.

I wanted to write and thank you for taking care of them.

Ever since a friend introduced me to your Fourteenth Street helping center the day of your annual Christmas dinner for the homeless a few years ago, I've been grateful that you're a part of the community I live in. Now, of course, I know you do so much more than Christmas and Easter and Thanksgiving dinner: the kids' after-school program and computer learning center; summer camp; McKenna's Wagon to feed the homeless on the District's streets every day; the clothing, bedding, towels and other items that find their way from your reception area to those who need them; your Christmas gift "store," where parents who are having hard times can still make kids' holiday dreams come true and wrap them up too. I am touched every year when the call for Christmas surprises goes out, to note that, besides the ever-popular Barbie, you remind us that your customers need wrapping paper and cellophane tape too!

That's precisely the personal touch that makes Martha's Table so special. I know there are many worthy social-service organizations, even in our broke and broken city, but your graciousness makes yours, to me, one of a kind.

Thanks for your warm embrace of both the people who come to you in need and the people who come to you to volunteer. I'm grateful to you for the way you welcome volunteers—you really make people feel involved in the real life of this self-involved city.

Bless you for the compassion that created Martha's Table, and the energy that keeps it going even in the face of the usual financial challenges. Thank you for all you've done and all you do.

Sincerely,

Pam Janis

Dear Phil Condit,

A few summers ago, we met in your office when I thought I might be moving to Seattle to be your new speechwriter. I thought then that I really wanted the job. So, here's a note I never dreamed I'd write: Thank you for not hiring me.

Please don't get me wrong—I knew in that meeting that I'd love working for you and that, despite my airsickness problem, I'd enjoy getting to know the industry you've built your career in and so clearly have a passion for. The 777 had just been introduced when we met and your excitement about it excited me for what would have been a great new adventure, which had the added bonus of being located in your gorgeous part of the country. What's seven or eight months of bad hair days when a Seattle summer finally comes calling?

I was sorry I didn't get the job.

But, as it turned out, good things happened when (maybe because?) I didn't. Other great writing opportunities came along for me, and I was grateful to be available to explore them. I'm a steely believer that everything happens for a reason, no matter how bummed out and mad and *sure* we are that the universe has made a mistake. As my Grandpa Jack used to say, "Baloney." There are no cosmic mistakes. Put it this way: a plane is grounded only to be overhauled and made ready to soar again.

Even the worst disappointment makes you available for new experiences, jobs, lovers, friends, causes and passions you might otherwise not even have noticed. The only difference between a setback and a change of course is one's attitude.

So while I wasn't delighted when Boeing said, "No, thanks" to me, I'm saying "Thanks" now. I feel lucky to have met you anyway and to have shared our ideas on both writing and aerospace. I've since flown on the 777, from San Francisco to Chicago most recently, and feel a real sense of appreciation, knowing how much it means to all the people who have worked on it.

I'm grateful to Boeing, too, for all the travels I've taken and people I've met, thanks to its planes. Since my first plane trip (TWA, New York to London) when I was fourteen, I've marveled at this great machine that makes no place too distant to delight in and no friend too far away forever. Boeing's planes have connected my life by the dots of its most joyous and challenging far-flung events: weddings, funerals, vacations, business trips, trysts and job interviews.

This isn't the copy I'd hoped to be writing for you a few summers ago, but I'm so glad I can make this a personal note. My thanks to you and every Boeing employee for making the airplanes that both wing me away and bring me home.

I have to confess I was a little relieved that I didn't get the job, for two reasons: first, because I wasn't sure in my heart that I was supposed to travel far from journalism (which proves to me that we eventually end up where our hearts, not our jobs, take us); and second, because the job involved a lot of travel (duh—this is *Boeing*), and I was a little nervous about maxing out on Dramamine. (Whenever I board a plane, I think of my Grandpa Jack's great line:

"The whole world is sick, and I'm not feeling so well myself.")

So, as it turned out, the silver lining behind every cloud isn't always a Boeing. Not landing the job allowed me to take off in another direction.

But I'm grateful for the chance I had to learn about your company and your leadership of it.

Thank you for a memorable meeting and career crossroads.

Sincerely,

Pam Janis

Dearest Larry, dearest friend,

Thank you for introducing me to the concept of eating grapefruit in sections.

Thank you for letting me cry on your couch and your shoulder when that guy didn't love me back.

Thank you for loving reading newspapers and writing for them and teaching me so much about both.

Thank you for helping me appreciate the, shall we say, politically conservative point of view. I think we've had some of our best discussions when we don't agree.

Thank you for good conversation, always.

And silliness.

Thank you for inviting me to your birthday dinner at Cities, when I wondered whether you were bringing a date and it turned out to be me.

Thank you for showing me that ridiculous headline you'd written in St. Petersburg for the moon landing. If I need a laugh, "Moon, We're Onto You" usually does it.

Thank you for the countless lattes at Starbucks while we tried to figure out whether our writing careers were equally stalled or equally full of promise.

Thank you for bringing Phil, Amy, Kitty, and Mimi into my life.

Thank you for being your uncompromising self and, in so doing, showing me that relationships can be maddeningly enigmatic at first, but then abiding and treasured.

Thank you for all the laughs.

Thank you for listening.

Thank you for confiding in me.

Thank you for your always insightful counsel.

Thank you for ten years and counting of sometimes romantic, sometimes platonic, sometimes journalistic, sometimes silly, sometimes literary, sometimes local, sometimes long-distance, sometimes side-by-side, sometimes arm in arm, sometimes by phone, sometimes by e-mail, sometimes by voice mail, sometimes by postcard and letter, never out of touch, always enduring love and friendship.

Love,

*P*am

Dear Alan Fisk, bubbie,

Never in six thousand years of Jewish history would I have believed that my reentry into newspaper journalism after wearing pantyhose, heels and little suits would come via a phone call from an editor in Detroit, twelve years and four hundred miles away from the scene of the last crime I covered.

If I'd had you for an editor the first time around, I might never have strayed from the fold (above it or otherwise). Not because you so brilliantly condense and unravel my more complex sentences—although you do—but because you really are one of the world's warmest, sweetest and most hilarious humans.

It's amazing to me that our editorial collaboration began on the phone before our first face-to-face meeting more than a year later. By then, you were a *londsman*, one of my *mishpacha*.

So, first, thank you for calling me to see if I'd like to write for the *News* after Marty Fischhoff made you. (Thanks, Marty, for reading my *USA Weekend* essay and thinking of me as a *News* freelancer.)

Then thank you for your skillful and wise editing and especially your gift for keeping a writer's voice in her story despite space, layout, play and all the rest of daily journalism's inevitable challenges and limits.

Then thank you for assigning me stories about my lifelong loves, books and authors. And for defending my review of that blech book by that egomaniac author when her husband threatened to sue. "Remind him that commentary is opinion," you told me. "Then give him my number, and I will too."

Then thank you for hearing my pitch to cover a pet-products trade show dressed like a cat. And then letting me. And then meowing on my answering machine for weeks afterward. Like I wouldn't know who it was.

I've never had so much freedom or fun writing the essays that I love to write best. I'm grateful to you and everyone in *The News*'s Accent section for making room for me in its pages and to the copy desk, which tweaks what I file and you edit.

And thank you, too, for listening to all my *bubba mysas,* including Tales from the Dating Crypt, and for telling me that the hit-on-and-runs are all out of their respective minds. Although I did *not* appreciate that conversation we had about the meteor that was mistakenly reported as likely to crash into Earth in 2025. (Don't believe everything you read in the newspaper.) We were surmising what we both might be doing when it hit, and you said, "You'll be on a date."

Thank you very much.

Love,

Your favorite freelancer

Dear Clairol, Clinique, and Lancôme,

Let's just keep this between ourselves, but thanks for all the help.

Sincerely,

X

Dear Debbie,

Yours was the most unusual baby shower I've ever been to for two reasons: 1) Because 60 of your customers showed up knowing you were pregnant with twins, the about-to-be-mommy had 120 gifts to open; and 2) Most of us were having the same bad hair day, because we hadn't let anyone else take scissors or blow dryer to our heads since you'd left on maternity leave. Who could blame us? One trip to you, and no woman can go back in hair-time.

Oh, Debbie, how can I ever thank you for rescuing me from a lifetime of monstrous haircapades? Let me hit the highlights:

° There was the literal highlight disaster when that woman in McLean who never used deodorant (why was she in a job that positions armpits over faces?; she must hate people) "cellophaned" my "streaks" "burgundy." That was the plan. The reality: my entire head was purple down to my scalp for months. I couldn't wear half my clothes; they didn't match my head.

  Such was my distress that first awful night at home alone, looking like a corporate executive gone punk, that I called my friend Dave Leonard at two in the morning with an SOS (Save Our Scalp). "My hair is grape," I told him. "I didn't know who else to call." The Nuclear Regulatory Commission would have been a good choice. The salon offered to color my hair again, free. Did they think I was out of my mind? Can't imagine why they went out of business.

° There was the time in New Jersey when, as a broke and time-pressed reporter, I went to a salon in the mall as a walk-in, and they gave me to a new hire, a former financier named Ivan who'd made a career change. Ivan was truly Terrible. His midlife crisis was my Mr. Spock look.

○ Once, when I was making good money (not as a reporter), I headed for Washington's most exclusive, pricey, status-y salon at the time. Its proprietor "did" Nancy Reagan; that should have been a warning to me. Needless to say, he didn't "do" me; that honor went to an apparently Pygmalion-obsessed underling who fashioned me in his own image. Today we'd call it Urban Paramilitary. I think what happened on P Street was best summed up by my friend and co-worker at the time, Scott Maclay, who passed my desk on the way into his office the next day, doubled back for another look and, considering, said, "Maybe you should wear really big earrings for a while."

○ Of course the trauma started in childhood with my father's Home Barber Kit. I can't even talk about it.

Okay, so where do you come in? I believe it was in the early '90s, just after that ditz in Bethesda dyed my eyebrows to match my experimental blonde highlights. My fault; I knew she was young enough to still be doing science projects. Grade: Incomplete.

In complete exasperation, root-weary, follicle-dazed, scalp-heavy, I stumbled into Lord & Taylor's, Chevy Chase. I think it was the only place in the tri-state area I hadn't yet written a check for a month's worth of bad hair days. I felt like Phyllis Diller, who once said, "When I go to the beauty parlor, I always use the emergency entrance. Sometimes I just go for an estimate."

Whoever worked the reception desk back then said

they'd "give" me to Debbie Dodsworth Lessin. I wondered if that meant Debbie Dodsworth Lessin, whoever she was, was on probation.

How do you do it? Okay, I now know I have to keep it all the same length, except for the feather bangs. You've told me the secret's in the sectioning, but when I try to blow it dry that way at home, it still looks as though my hair and I should be in counseling.

So I've come to the conclusion, finally, that I'm not supposed to know what you do or how you do it. It's enough that I found you. You're magical.

How else to explain your beating the fertility odds, after hormone-heavy months of disappointment and discouragement, ending with your own dearest, most magical wish not only coming true but doubling?

Some of your customers' hair may look like hell for a while, but I'll bet Austin's and Jessica's look great.

Thank you for the years so far of great haircuts, patient blow-drying and deft styling, and especially for sharing all the friendship, news and views that have filled the grateful hours I've spent in the chair at your station.

Love,

Pam J.

Dear Inge Windig,

I can't believe I'm thanking someone for slathering hot wax across certain parts of my face and then ripping it off, but if it must be done (and it must), there's no one I'd rather have do it than you.

Thank you for making my brow and mouth areas look less like my cat's.

    With gratitude,

    Pam J.

Dear Jeanne Thurow,

Callie (Puss) is batting around one of those too-realistic-for-comfort rabbity-furred mice even as I write this letter to you from Calistoga, California, her ancestral home, so if you suddenly see a bfjhbsbuwevhcvajuenfnnfnmgiofu in the middle of this page, it means she tried to jump over me after it and landed on the keyboard.

It's happened before.

Nevertheless, I'm writing to thank you for her.

If you hadn't answered my personal ad—"WOMAN SEEKS CAT"—in the weekly *Calistogan* in March of 1991, I might have had to find an East Coast kitty after all, which would have missed the point of Callie entirely.

What *was* the point of going to California to cart home a cat? People ask me this all the time. My answer—the true story—has become sort of a first-date test: does he get it? If he says, "Oh, I see," but doesn't, it's time for the next contestant.

Because putting a call into the universe isn't supposed to make any more sense than having it returned. Some things are just supposed to happen. Who knows why they actually do?

But since I can't remember if I ever told *you* how the ad came about, here's the story:

My dear chum Toots, who lives in San Francisco, first brought me to Calistoga in the mid-'80s, when she moved out here. It became our special place. So, when she told me she was pregnant with her first child, Matthew, I decided to come see her for one last pre-kid time just before she was due. Then I decided I wanted not a baby, too, but something a little more my speed, some form of company and unconditional love that wouldn't wig me out for the next eighteen years, say, a cat or a Volvo.

A cat seemed a more likely bedmate for me (this is why my mother worries), as well as a cousin for Toots's child (although it turns out Matthew is allergic to cats). Then I thought, Well, why don't I just get a cat in Calistoga while I'm out there, to commemorate both Toots's special time and our special place.

There are two things I love in both writing and life: metaphors and subplots. The subplot in this case was that I was a corporate speechwriter at the time and wanted a companion who would truly complement my life, which was then composed mainly of oratory and wordplay. So I needed either a persuasive plant or an alliterative animal.

Thus the call was put in to the universe for a Calico Cat from Calistoga, California.

Toots and I composed the newspaper ad you answered—display, I want you to know, above-the-fold on page 3; I knew the universe wouldn't find me if I was lost in the classifieds. Fifty bucks to run for two Thursdays. It was Toots who wrote the line, "Cat must be willing to relocate."

I wanted to give the universe a second choice just in case it was out of calico (this is what happens when you're a Lands' End recidivist), so I listed gray, too. Then we put the ad Out There.

And *you* called me!

"Pam," you said. "My name is Jeannie. I think I might have your cat." And you proceeded to tell me about the gray-and-white kitten your son had rescued on Lincoln Avenue, Calistoga's main street, the previous Halloween when a man with four kittens in a box told passersby that those he hadn't given away by nightfall would be destroyed. Your son plucked Puss, as he called her, out of harm's way and brought her home. The only problem was, Puss and the rottweilers you'd also rescued were getting along about as well as Rodney King and the LAPD.

So Puss had been living in the garage, but it was cold in Lake County, and you knew she couldn't stay there. Enter your kids again, who read my ad and told you, "Mom, you should call this woman." (Thanks, Wells kids.)

You were so charming when you called—you wanted me to see Polaroids of Puss first to avoid cat adopter's remorse. Two days later the Polaroids arrived in the mail, Puss wearing her "You're wearing *that*?" look, which, by the way, she's never lost, so either this cat has an attitude or I have truly ghastly taste in clothes.

Here's something I've never told you in my Christmas cards since: remember how when Callie (my name for her) got her shots at the vet's that day, he told me to have her boosters done a month later? So, exactly a month later, I took Callie to her vet, Dr. Lynne Cabaniss, to take care of that and also to have Lynne do a pre-spay exam.

Lynne vaccinated her, then palpated her belly.

"Is this cat pregnant?" she asked.

"Nope, impossible. She doesn't go out."

"I think this cat is pregnant. . . . There are three kittens in here," Lynne said.

It was the day before Mother's Day. All I could think was, "Okay, you guys, who's responsible for this, Toots or the universe?"

Lynne palpated some more.

"She's about thirty days pregnant, I'd say."

"No, can't be, I've had her a month."

Then I calculated.

"I've had her for twenty-nine days!"

Well, there was no way any of us could have known. As my friend Dave Leonard said when he heard the story (which I shrieked to him over the phone the minute Puss and Grandma got home), "Must have been the going-away party."

I didn't have the heart to tell you, because unfortunately the kittens weren't born (Callie had had two rounds of lethal-to-fetus vaccinations by then). I'm telling you now because I don't want her calling you up someday and saying, "Hi, I'm the cat you put up for adoption, and you wouldn't believe what that witch you left me with did to my kittens."

I have reason to worry about things like this with Callie. She once told an animal telepathist in Houston who I was interviewing on the phone for a *Detroit News* story—after first stepping on the phone, disconnecting us—that she hates it when I don't tell her what time I'm coming home, and could I please use the blue dish all the time for supper instead of rotating bowls based on what's clean because blue's her favorite color? (Oh, how I wish I *were* making this up.) Since then, I've paid stricter attention to her chatty chirps and meows.

She can talk your ear off, but she's great company curled next to me on the couch as I type on my laptop computer during the day, and curled inside the curve of my hips on the bed as I lie under its comforter at night. So many good things have happened in my writer's life since Callie joined it that I'm convinced she's something more than a cat. My friend Pam Vennerdrow calls her a "cat-alyst."

In the seven years since I put my ad Out There and you answered it, Jeanne, Callie–Puss has been not only by my side but inside that kennel in my heart that's reserved for the animals entrusted to my care. She was preceded by my great growing-up black multi-breed dog, Curly, and the three sable ferrets, Connie, Chloe and Reuben. (The ferrets were metaphors rather than subplots; I was a reporter at the time.)

I'm convinced that our animals are "assigned" to us to bring joy, companionship, comfort and fun at different times of our lives. (The universe seems to send me ones that mirror my natural hair color at the time too. I wonder what would happen if Callie got into my Loving Care.)

When she's not criticizing my taste or complaining about me to the authorities, we're the best of friends. Sometimes I'm not sure whether she's another person or I'm another cat.

I love my Callie co-cat from Calistoga, California.

Thank you, Jeanne, for delivering her to me from the bnfjhbsbuwevhcvajuenfnfnmgiofuiihdnmcmvnmvnmvnvnvmv mvmmmmmmnf universe.

Sincerely,

Woman Who Sought Cat

TO: LYNNE CABANISS, D.V.M.
    COLLINS MEMORIAL ANIMAL HOSPITAL
    WASHINGTON, D.C.

Dear Lynne,

I can't imagine a better veterinarian for my darlings—
first the ferrets, now Callie—than you.

Thanks for the thorough, skilled and compassionate way
you've tended to them in their growing-up (and, in the
ferrets' cases, growing-old) years.

I will probably never stop asking you what certain of
their behaviors mean, if only to hear again your answer,
"I'm a veterinarian, not a psychic."

I'll never forget how you had me bring Reuben to the
office the day we had to put Chloe down, because, you
said, "Animals understand death. They don't understand
when their friend just doesn't come home."

He sniffed, and he understood.

Thank you for taking such great care of them—and me.

Love,

Pam

Dear Kathy Balog,

Congratulations: you are the only friend I've ever argued with so viciously that we sometimes had to flounce off, each of us in sullen silence, for all of about, say, fifteen minutes, before one of us got over it first. And considering we met teaming up on a magazine freelance job in crowded quarters, our more incendiary days were tough for everyone. Did you really have to refer to that mini plaid skirt as my "Spank Me Catholic Schoolgirl" outfit? You're right most of the time, but not *all* the time, Missy, and since I'm hardly ever right all of the time, I say we call it a draw once again and go out for a couple of Sabrett hot dogs from the street vendor on the Gannett corner. Because I never want to stop thanking you for either eating carny midway food with me—or keeping me honest.

Love,

Pam

P.S.: I look *great* in that skirt, and you know it.

Dear Tony Wood,

Hi, remember me from Kenyon?

I just wanted to thank you for the great wedding toast you gave as best man at Jerry and Lena's wedding. (Yes, I'm a speechwriter, but one of the things speechwriters do best is steal—I mean, borrow—good material.)

I've used this toast not only at weddings myself but in speeches I've written for others. Your toast was:

> "May the most that you wish for be the least that you achieve."

I just love that.

Thanks for saying it so well.

> Sincerely,
>
> *Pam Janis*

Dear Rosie,

I'd be starting this letter "Dear ATMs" if your employer had had its way, because you once told me they wanted more of your branch's customers to use the money machines. Apparently Citibank's senior management noticed that the ATM use was down when real people were working in the branch and couldn't figure out why. They assembled the friendliest, most personal "personal bankers" money could buy, so to speak, then wondered why we preferred to visit with them instead of an ATM!

Because you're the main reason I mostly skipped "electronic banking" during the branch's business hours before you retired, I'm writing to thank *you,* even though Citibank itself and I go way back—two decades, to be precise, since my friend Vicki and I had our first apartment in New York.

I actually chose Citibank for my first account as a working adult *because* they had those then-newfangled ATMs. In 1977, anyone who knew my boyfriend's name knew my PIN, and breaking up meant a trip into the Third at 61st Street branch to make it official. In this way, I got through M-A-R-K, then wondered whether M-I-C-H-A-E-L was PIN-worthy or just a summer thing, and held out for A-N-D-R-E-W. What would I have done if I'd ever met a guy with fewer than four or more than eight letters in his name—Lee, say, or Alexander?

It was prescient of Citibank to soon call a halt to my ATM dating diary by assigning random-number PINs. If they feared system overload, imagine mine: I've been dating for twenty years.

Yikes—I just realized that this means my longest intimate relationship has been with a bank.

There's a reason for that, and it has to do with you.

Rosie, do you realize what a delight it is to find a sincere, friendly, positive and truly helpful "service" person anywhere, let alone an impersonal "financial institution"? You gave the information counter a whole new meaning, because you didn't just give information out; you took it in. I heard you ask customers about their spouses and houses—you remembered when those single checking accounts went joint and when that mortgage was taken out. You asked about people's health—you noticed when someone came in with a prescription bag from the CVS pharmacy three corners down. You followed your customers' stories from deposits to withdrawals, loans to paybacks.

When you asked me, "How's your writing?," I felt like I was at Cheers, not Citibank.

Even though it's the place where everybody *does* know your name (because it's printed on your checks), no amount of customer-service training in the world can make a Rosie Richards. Your friendly interest in people came from the heart, not the bank's policy manual.

So thank you, first, for understanding that freelancers' "payroll" checks come from many different employers and that we're only on the "payroll" on a per-story, -speech or -script basis. Without your understanding—and your initials—freelancers like me couldn't deposit our checks as cash.

Thank you, also, for periodically explaining this to confused new tellers who didn't see my "Good Customer Profile" right away.

Thank you, too, for being the first person ever to ask for my autograph, not to endorse a check but on one of my *Washington Post* stories. (The only thing I've ever signed at Citibank that didn't show up on my next monthly statement.) You had me smiling for days with that one.

It's genuine gestures like this that made your customers in the Citibank branch at 5700 Conn. Ave. feel like a million bucks, even when they were making substantially less.

As one of them, I thank you.

Sincerely,

That woman writer with the Bugs Bunny checks

Dear Alan Alda,

The closest I've come to meeting you was at a Chinese restaurant at Broadway and 96th in 1980. I was sitting with a circle of friends, from Columbia probably, and hearing your voice fusing with ours. They must be watching *M*A*S*H* in the kitchen, I thought. They should turn it down. Then I realized it was *you* I was hearing, at the table next to ours, also in a circle of friends, and whatever else had been in my head flew out of there like a *M*A*S*H* chopper.

I was too surprised and shy to do that night what, later, I wished I had, which is thank you for both my particular favorite Alan Alda movie, *Same Time, Next Year*, and of course *M*A*S*H*.

So I want to thank you now.

Same Time, Next Year: What a great story! I couldn't imagine anyone but you playing that part. Loved it when I saw it for the first time in New York with my friend Vicki Barker. Still do, when I rent it.

Thanks for the movie.

As many good movies as you've made, though, I've never been as emotional about them as I am (because it's still in reruns) about *M*A*S*H*. In fact, I've never been as emotional about *any* TV show as I am about *M*A*S*H*. It's a jumble as to why: because it's the Korean War my dad served in; because it's the Vietnam War that was still going on when the show began; because Henry died in that chopper crash on his way home; because B.J. missed Peg and Erin so much; because futility and hopelessness were constantly at war with small triumphs and rays of hope; because my arms and wrists were pretty much disabled for more than a year beginning in August of 1992 from carpal tunnel syndrome and during that awful time the only thing I looked forward to was WTTG Fox Channel 5's *M*A*S*H* hour at 11:30 P.M.

Experiencing chronic pain and depression that year, I stayed up late every night watching *M*A*S*H*, remembering the episodes I'd seen when they were first on and memorizing the ones I hadn't. I realized that I'd missed whole years of the show the first time around, depending on what was going on in my life at the time, and that I'd gotten it but I really hadn't *gotten it* when I watched it in my teens and twenties.

Thanks to Channel 5's doubling up on the episodes five nights a week, I saw the show cycle from Henry to Colonel Potter, Trapper to B.J., Frank to Charles, Radar in the office to Klinger in the office, Margaret as Hot Lips to Margaret as mature and sensitive, the first episode to the penultimate episode (they never show the final episode when the war ends in reruns; they take it only to the time-capsule episode) more times than I can count.

Thank you for *M*A*S*H*'s brilliance and poignancy, and yours, too, as Hawkeye. For you, the show might be a career and life's episode that began 25 years ago, but for those of us still watching it, it's part of today too. Only some of the first couple of seasons' episodes seem dated—the doctor/nurse relationship story lines, mostly—otherwise, it's as enduring as your father Robert Alda's voice on the great original Broadway-cast recording of *Guys and Dolls,* for which I thank *him.*

That year my hands were mostly disabled, I felt that

I, too, was trying to patch up chaos and insanity and terror (Would I ever work as a writer again? How could I not—it wasn't just what I *did*; it was who I *was*. Could God let this happen?) along with the *M*A*S*H* doctors and nurses. The show's most profound and sobering plotlines would remind me that we tell stories—in TV shows, in books, in movies and plays, in art—to organize the jumbled drawers of life. Only then can we hope to clearly see what's really in there and realize what's valuable and important— critical, even—to living in the world and what can be tossed.

I remember reading excerpts of your commencement address to Columbia's med school in *TIME Magazine* one year and marveling that you, an actor who played a doctor on TV, spoke of the compassion and responsibility those new doctors must be mindful of feeling toward those they helped if their help was to be truly meaningful. I hope they took your words to heart.

M*A*S*H's most comic plots and moments would remind me that there's funny stuff out there even when you're feeling your worst and that there is no end to the human imagination's surprises.

Thanks for doctoring me back to health that year.

The night the last *M*A*S*H* was shown, I watched it with my friend Martha Goodwin in her Falls Church apartment. It was so powerful, such a boldface period on *M*A*S*H*'s eleven-season run, that I've never been able to bring myself to rent it since.

You, Larry Gelbart, the brilliant cast and writers and all of *M*A*S*H*'s other creators made something extraordinary happen from 1972 to 1983, and I wanted to let you know how grateful and affected I am that you did.

Thank you for the show.

Sincerely,

Pam Janis

P.S.: I think of that time I saw you in the Chinese restaurant as a reminder not to let an opportunity to thank someone go by.

Dear Futuro and Mylan Laboratories Inc.,

I hate having to need you, but I'm grateful to you.

You're the makers of the wrist braces I need to sleep in and the medication I need to take to head off at the pass at least some of carpal tunnel and chronic fatigue syndromes' more difficult symptoms.

This is a huge drag, having to deal with a body that occasionally short-circuits, let me tell you. But the good news is that thanks to both your companies, what began as a full-scale power outage now just means a periodic brownout.

Since I've had these complementary inconveniences, I've moved from anger at losing my perfect health to gratitude at having good health most of the time and having the means to handle setbacks.

It's really a whole new way of looking at the givens for me. (Of course, I still hope it will all go away someday; I'm not *that* centered.)

But since these are the hands I've been dealt, so to speak, I'm so grateful to have the resources to soothe them. While I wouldn't wish a repetitive stress injury or CFS on my worst enemy, now that I have both, I'm grateful for everything that helps me manage them.

So thanks to you both.

Sincerely,

Pam Janis

Dear McNEIL–PPC, Inc., Ft. Washington, PA,

God makes all things possible, but Lactaid is a close second.

Thank you for making and distributing it.

Sincerely,

Your best customer

cc: Ben & Jerry's
Dove Bars
Haagen Dazs
Good Humor
Baskin-Robbins
Starbucks
Philadelphia Cream Cheese
Silver Diner, Milkshakes Department
France

Dear Kathy Stumpe,

Before you made TV watchers laugh, you made me laugh, and I'm writing to thank you.

When we were kids and used to cut through the woods that connected our neighborhoods, you were my favorite friend. I was stealing material from you when we were nine. There was, for instance, that stupid TV commercial with the "Girlwatchers" music that showed a series of guys on a beach, following curvy women in bikinis with their eyes. The voice-over began, "Half the world are girlwatchers. . . ."

The first time we saw it together, you broke right in: "The other half are girls. . . ."

"That's very funny," my father told me when *I* said it, timing it the way you had.

This is the way it went: you'd say something funny and sophisticated, and then I'd go home and try it on my parents.

So naturally, you grew up to write sitcoms, and I grew up to write speeches.

I missed you so much when your family moved to Milwaukee in junior high. I can't believe we didn't write! Thanks to you, I write (or call or e-mail) everyone I know who lives far away. I just couldn't go through another twenty-five-year period of wondering, Whatever happened to . . . ? Especially with as important a chum to me as you were.

But here's the funny part: I always knew I'd find you again, somewhere in life. So was it really a coincidence that, after twenty-five years of not knowing where you were, and a couple of seasons of my having missed *Cheers*, I tuned in to the last episode?

I saw the name on the closing credits just long enough to realize two things: you were now officially "Kathy Ann Stumpe," and *"I found her!"*

The news was confirmed the next day by a woman at Paramount who said, "Did your childhood friend have red hair?"

Thanks for remembering me when I called. (*"The white go-go boots!"* you shouted.)

Now that you're back in my life, I realize how quick and sure is the intuitive knowledge kids have about people and especially other kids. When my mother heard the *Cheers* story, she said, "What are the chances you'd both turn out to be writers?" But to me, remembering how it felt to be with a kindred spirit after school and on weekends, it seems inevitable.

So thank you, my long-ago childhood friend, for the giggles you supplied while our destinies were hatching. And for the lesson that people who are supposed to find each other in life do . . . maybe even twice.

Love,

Pam

P.S.: I did tell my dad it was you who said that about the other half of the world being girls.

P.P.S.: I'm really sorry I hurt your feelings when I was mean about red hair that time we were playing Barbies.

Dear Michele one "l,"

I know my first reaction to the news of your planned arrival when I was four wasn't very welcoming. Mom swears my exact words to her were, "That's ridiculous. You just had Caroline."

Thanks for being my best friend for most of the last thirty-seven years in spite of that.

It's funny; I really can't remember when we went from being sisters who were friends to friends who are sisters.

You've been listening and making me laugh for as long as I can remember. I get tears in my eyes cracking up over stories you told me more than twenty years ago, like the time you were thirteen and went on your first date with What's-Her-Name's brother. Neither of you had any idea what *Hair* was about. Remember what he squeaked out in the awkward intermission silence after act 1? I do: "Wanna . . . Sprite?"

Thank you for entertaining me with reports of all the loser dates you went on in your twenties—before Bobby married you in what amounted to an intervention. How we howled over them! The guy who, over dessert at Belmont Kitchen, raked his *schmutzy* fingers through the table sugar bowl. The guy who sent you a "report card" on how you did on a date with him, giving you a 6 for humor and a 10 for "humor appreciation." The guy who told you he liked to vacation alone, then took off for a week with his next girlfriend.

I don't think resigning my diaphragm in protest over that one was too generous an act on your behalf. You know this is true: when you got done telling me and my then-roommate, Vicki, the story, I got up, yelled, *"I quit!,"* grabbed my diaphragm from the bathroom and ran to the end of the hall, where I threw it in the incinerator.

You're that sort of sister.

Thank you for insisting that I overcome my innate disdain for Disney World and making me go with you when you met me in Orlando that time I was there for a conference. I do *not* thank you for taking me on the teacups ride. I think I probably told you how I really felt about that when I came to. I still have the picture of us waving in front of the Magic Kingdom in the little green frame on my dresser, two joyous kindergarteners in their thirties. You told the ticket agents at the airport that we had to bring those helium Mickey balloons on board with us or there'd be "two very disappointed little girls back in Washington."

Coming up with a spin like that on the spot is why you're such a *macher* in P.R. today. Remember how we watched in horror as those balloons swelled and swelled and swelled under the seats in front of us, knowing we were going to be in Big Trouble any minute? When they *finally* exploded, so did we—in laughter.

I've never met another woman who could capture a caper in a line like you. For God knows what reason, we just had to go to the circus six years ago. High up in the bleachers, we watched as a hypnotist manipulated a trained alligator, which crawled out of a box and crept toward the edges of the ring. You turned toward me and said, "That reminds me. I need shoes."

You hated your beautiful, naturally curly hair growing up, but boy, did you luck out in the tush department. I'll never forget the time I was stopped at a light at M and Connecticut, saw a woman in a tricolored striped business dress cross the street, and thought, Man, that woman has a great butt. Then I realized it was you.

You're the person everyone always wants to sit next to. When my friends became your friends somewhere along the way and our four-year age difference disappeared everywhere but my gray hair roots, that's when I realized that we'd be best friends even if we hadn't been sisters.

Thank you for the roses and cards to celebrate my successes and all the consolation for my disappointments. Thank you for listening to me not just when things are going great but when they're bad, unfair, crazy, miserable, or just plain suck. Thank you for all the things I don't want to write in a letter but you know what they are. Thank you for your enduring loyalty and knowing what both the thrills and the chills of my life really *mean* to me.

When I think about not only how we grew up together as kids but how we've grown together as women, I get misty. I hope this doesn't sound too pathetic, but your wedding day was one of the happiest days of *my* life.

And now you're a new mom. As you say, "This is *big*."

"Look at this," you said to me in your and Bobby's bedroom one night in your seventh month after we'd eaten Thai. "You've got to see this." Stripping, you demonstrated first the back—the normal Michele—then the front—the pregnant Michele. We stared at what you'd been watching change every day since September 1, your birthday, the day my gorgeous niece Shoshi first announced her officiality by making you puke. (For the first time. "If it's a boy, we'll have to name him Ralph," you said in your fifth month.)

"Pam, it's amazing," you said, showing me your Mickey-balloon-on-the-plane stomach. "We're born with all this software, but we have no idea what it can do until you click on the application."

That's my sister Michele.

How lucky I am to have you as both a best friend and a blood relative. How lucky I am to share both the sobs and belly laughs of life with a sister who not only really *gets* those special and important three little words but says them, often, and hears them from me, often. I don't mean "Don't tell Mom"; I mean "I love you."

Thanks for being you and, by being you, being the best friend I'll ever have.

Love,

Pam

Dear Rabbi Laszlo Berkowits,

I can hardly believe you've retired from Temple Rodef Shalom; you *are* Temple Rodef Shalom to me.

The thank-yous are coming from the whole congregation, I know, but I wanted to personally express my gratitude to you because I have considered you a special friend since our first meeting in the fall of 1982, when I moved to Washington from New Jersey.

You were my mother's rabbi, first; I laughed when I heard she joined a temple in Falls *Church*. I was between jobs at the time and had come home thinking I'd bank a little rent-free R-and-R time with Mom before sending out resumes. But I needed something to do in the meantime, and the temple was looking for religious schoolteachers, so I decided to check it out.

I'll be honest; I would have thought I'd be the last person to teach Sunday school.

I *mean* because I'm a late sleeper, and school staffers had to be there by 8:15 A.M.

But I signed on anyway, and I'm so glad I did.

As I got to know you over that year and heard your powerful story as a Holocaust survivor, I was first moved by your gratitude for life's Source and your own life and then began to truly feel grateful for *mine*.

You, a man who takes nothing for granted, whose every word and action are heartfelt, taught not only my fifth graders but me that year that the human soul and spirit are as enduring as every moment is fleeting.

I think of your life's experience, so different from those northern Virginia ten-year-olds as to be laughable. Their growing-up years were being spent shuttling between soccer fields and the Discovery Zone; as a boy, you were hustled from your native Derecske in Hungary into the Auschwitz II and Wobbelin Nazi slave-labor camps. Your parents, sister and brother were murdered in Auschwitz and Birkenau.

Yet it wasn't a sad, scary story that you told. Exuding light, you made the kids and their teacher understand that you felt blessed by God for having survived the darkness that made Him cry too.

You told me at another time that when your camp was liberated by the U.S. Army's 82nd Airborne Division on May 2, 1945, the survivors were sent to Hälsingborg, Sweden. As you began to see land streak across the horizon from your place on the ship's packed deck, you felt touched—"kissed," you said—by God Himself and knew in that moment that you must become a rabbi. Almost as instantly as it came upon you, you related, that holy moment of perfection and oneness began to ebb.

But, you said, its message for the rest of your life was loud and clear.

Once when I was engrossed in a writing project on trauma survivors, you phoned to remind me not to get so involved in the subject that I'd forget to laugh and play and celebrate the world's enjoyments.

Thank you, Rabbi Berkowits, for making the call and answering the Calling.

Love,

Pam

*To the unknown male resident in George Washington
University Hospital's radiology department on duty the morning
of September 16, 1996,*

I tried to find out who you were to thank you by
name, but they said it wasn't in my records.

So, whoever you are, thank you for coming into the
waiting anteroom to tell me personally that everything was
fine and that the second mammogram was clear. There
was, you said, no sure explanation for the shadow on the
first. Sorry we called you on Friday and you had to wait
until Monday to do this, you said. You're fine!

As my mother once said to a beau who'd dumped her
thirty years before but upon seeing her again said it felt
like just a weekend ago, *"That was some weekend you gave
me."*

So before I thank you—and God—for my being fine, I
want to tell you what it's like to be forty and one of nine
women, as I was, waiting together to have mammograms,
however routine, scheduled or baseline they are.

You think of the statistics: one in nine women . . . one
of *us*. You think of the women you know, your relations,
friends, friends of friends, friends' relations, work
colleagues, everyone you've ever heard of who is in various
stages of treatment for, recovery of or decline from breast
cancer.

You think of everyone else you know or knew who has
or had some form, any form, of cancer.

You think of one of your gay male friends asking you
once while watching a *Nightline* edition on AIDs together,
"Are you as afraid of breast cancer as I am of this?"

You think of how short your life will have been if . . .

But then you think how great it's been too. Wonderful, in fact. Magical. So much to be thankful for. *You couldn't have gotten luckier.*

That, at least, is what I was thinking.

Then you came in.

Thank you, Doctor, for telling me that I had, in fact, gotten luckier.

God bless you and every person waiting scared in an anteroom, especially those less lucky than I.

> *April 27, 1998*
> *Washington, D.C., and Calistoga,*
> *California*

More Thank-Yous

No author birthing a book could feel as lucky as I do. Between the lines on these pages are the love, support and help of many more wonderful family members, friends, helpers, clients, and angels in all forms than could be thanked within.

First, my deepest gratitude to my agent, Leslie Breed, whose talent, faith, confidence, and friendship mean the world to me. Thanks, Les, for believing and keeping me believing, too, that someday there would be a book with my name on it.

Thanks, too, to my editor at Avon Books, Tia Maggini, for her editing gifts and speed and her care with my written voice. Also at Avon Books, thanks to Ann McKay Thoroman, for first saying, "Yes."

Thanks to my mother, Lucille Janis Weener, and stepdad, Sumner Weener, for their support as I wrote this book and always. And thanks to my siblings, the other three of Mom's "four only children," Caroline, Michele and Gordon, for cheering me on all the way through, as did my sisters' spouses, Malcolm Rimmer and Bobby Levenson, and all my relatives on both the Janis and Goldfeder sides, including the Dr. Stefanie Halpern-Zevy, Arthur Feltheimer, Dr. Howard Bernstein and Herb Goldfeder families. Thanks to all of you!

A HUGE thank you goes to my Kenyon classmate, copyright attorney Noel M. Cook, and associate Linda J. Kattwinkel of Owen, Wickersham & Erickson, P.C. in San

Francisco for their generous and painstaking work on my manuscript.

Several dear friends—gifted journalists, all—read various incarnations of my manuscript and gave valuable counsel: thank you to Vicki Barker, Ann Grimes, Beth Levine and Kathy Seligman, and not just for reading my book, you Great Women.

Thank you to all the special people in my life who make up the village it took: Alma Rock Road's families from 1962–1980; Vicki's family, Joanne, Ruth (Mima) and A.J. Barker; Susan Levitan Barnes; Cathie Black and Tom Harvey; Marcia Broadway and Dave Leonard; Rev. Alma Daniel and K. Martin–Kuri for their spiritual guidance at an important time in my life; Caroline DeCesare and Rex Brown; Elsa; Ellen Murphy Freeman and Thomas P. Murphy; Sheila Gibbons and Ray Hiebert; Martha Goodwin; my lifelong RW1 buddies from Ken's class, Randi Londer Gould and Mary Ellin Lerner; Jeff Gottlieb; Paul Grimes, David Heiden; Susan Hooper; Celeste James; Larry Jolidon; Robin Kane; Judi and Frank Kauffman; the two speechwriting Bobs, Klear and Putnam, for their affection and support through our professional years; Phil Lerman; my fellow MADD Ladies Kathy Balog, Jeanne Wright and Carol Memmott for all the fun we've shared; Nancy and Dan Magida; Gary Markowitz; Burt and Rona Peck for their help with my 1992 transcenders project; Julie Pistone Pertz (coo); Alex Gordevich Rota; Mary Rumsey and Jim Dorskind; Julie, Schuyler, Peter and John Rumsey; Dr. Dolly Shaffer; the Shrewsbury, N. J. *Daily Register* staff of 1980–1982; Tom S. for waiting with me at G.W. that day; Anne Uno for her financial guidance through my freelance years; Pam Vennerdrow; and Carolyn and Bill Wheatley for their loyal friendship and support since my NBC days.

Thanks to these dear friends—and to borrow an expression from Vicki, "karmic wildcards"—my writing time in Calistoga, California, was magical: first and foremost, thank you to Jia Ness for placing the call from the universe, and a big, BIG thank you to Mary Wegars, who generously shared her home and her life with me and my cat, making my dream of writing the book in California come true.

Thanks to my Calistoga healing angel, Barbara Versage Bobsin and everyone at Indian Springs, and all of Calistoga's friendly people, including those at Calistoga Jewelers; Calistoga Pet Supply; the All Seasons and Sarafornia cafes; the Puerto Vallarta restaurant and the Calistoga Bookstore with its Cats! Cats! Cats! section. Thank you to Mary's book club and the Oscar Night ladies for welcoming me so warmly.

Also related to my California sojourn: Thank you to Dr. Kathy Kimber, D.V.M., for her help with Callie on the United flight to S.F. from O'Hare. And thanks to Dr. Mark and Nurse Denise, of Wilmington, Delaware's Christiana Hospital (I never did learn your last names), for being so nice after the overhead litter box mishap on the flight home.

Most speechwriters' clients prefer anonymity, but a heartfelt thanks to all of you who know who you are, for supporting this project from the start and giving me the time I needed to complete it. Thanks, too, to my other writing colleagues and friends who supported me throughout the process, including Paul Luthringer and Gloria Ricks at Hearst; Alan Fisk at the *Detroit News;* and my chums at *USA Weekend Magazine* and *USA Today*. Thank you, too, to all my friends at Gannett corporate, scene of my best "real" job ever, notably John Curley, members of the Public Affairs department and Newspaper Division, and Jose Berrios, for launching me into the post-corporate writing world with such solid backing and encouragement. My gratitude also goes to all my editorial, video, and other business clients of the past seven years who, by giving me work, made it possible for me to work toward becoming an author.

Special thanks go to Jodie Hawk for her make-up artistry and Debbie Dodsworth Lessin for her hair magic the day of the photo shoot. Thanks, Davey, for taking the photo. It had to be you!

My everlasting gratitude to Bonnie Raitt and Bruce Springsteen for both their very gracious and generous "Yesses" on the permissions front and their music, always.

Thank you to my J-school classmate James McBride, whose example inspired me and who once told me it's worth it to "endure discomfort" to write whatever it is that calls you. He's right. And thank you to James's mother, Ruth McBride Jordan, for writing *me* one of the all-time great thank-you notes I've ever received, which said, in part "Don't be afraid to take risks. God always provides."

She's right, too.

And, finally, a thank you to the tattered sage outside the Tenleytown McDonald's one day a few winters ago, who was overheard saying this to his equally ragged friend; quote:

"Every day you goddamn wake up is a holiday."

Thank you, everyone.